From Sensor Networks to Customer Clicks: How Online Learning Makes Sense of Real-Time Data

Sartre

Contents

Chapter 1

Introduction

Data streams are defined as large sequences of data, gathered from sources such as sensor networks and customer click streams, that are possibly infinite and temporarily ordered [7, 22]. Instances in data streams arrive fast, either in batches of data, or instance-by-instance; each instance needs to be processed in a timely manner. Due to these characteristics, such as large amount of data and time constraints, traditional static machine learning algorithms are unsuitable for direct use [7]. That is, techniques learning from data streams need to maintain their performance throughout the stream while limiting memory and processing time. Moreover, evolving or non-stationary data streams are susceptible to changes in the distribution of data, also known as concept drifts. In such situations, algorithms must be able to deal with these changes by, if appropriate, forgetting past knowledge and adapting the resultant models to focus on recent concepts [22]. These characteristics have led to developing online learning algorithms with wide applications across numerous domains. Thus, online supervised learning from streaming data is an active area of research with the objective of building near-real-time models capable of continuously adapting to the changes taking place in fast-evolving repositories.

1.1 Motivation

In real-world data streams, it is often the case that some classes appear more frequently than others. For instance, let us consider an application of data streams in detecting network intrusions, where the goal is to differentiate different types of intrusions (or attacks) from normal connections. In this stream, a high proportion of instances might involve normal connections, while a limited proportion of instances might be related to the different types of intrusions or attacks such as Denial-of-Service (DoS) or probe attacks [5]. In such cases, a classifier learning from the data might be biased towards the classes with the majority number of instances (majority classes), which could greatly reduce the performance of the classifier in classifying instances in the classes with the least number of instances (minority classes) [17, 37]. In our multi-class example, a classifier learning from the stream might be biased towards the class with normal connections, while detecting different intrusion classes might be more critical [5]. Overall, this problem is more formally defined as having an *imbalanced* data stream. When there are only two classes (one minority and one majority class), the problem is defined as online imbalanced binary classification, and when there are more than two (multiple minority or majority classes), the problem is defined as online multi-class imbalanced classification. Online imbalanced learning on binary classification has received considerable attention, while online multi-class imbalanced classification has received limited attention [17, 37].

Sampling methods are effective methods for dealing with the challenges associated with having imbalanced data that perform by either increasing the number of instances in the minority classes (over-sampling), decreasing the number of instances in the majority classes (under-sampling), or a combination of both over-sampling and under-sampling [17].

Current methods for dealing with online multi-class class imbalanced such as Multi-class Over-sampling Online Bagging (MOOB) and Multi-class Under-sampling Online Bagging (MUOB) only rely on sampling instances based on their frequency and do not consider the performance of the classifier for each class [71]. That is, these methods only over-sample the classes with the least frequent instances (MOOB), or under-sample classes with the highest number of instances (MUOB), while not considering the classifying performance of the classifier in each individual class. Other methods such as SCUT-DS [46] sample instances in each batch of data. In cases of highly imbalanced data, each batch can create an excessive number of synthetic instances, which could lower the algorithm's efficiency. However, sampling based on the frequency alone might not deal with the negative impacts caused by highly class imbalanced streams. For instance, in some multi-class imbalanced learning datasets, a classifier may still perform well on some minority classes, indicating that all classes do not need to be re-sampled. On the other hand, some classes might be more frequent, but the classifier trained on the data might have poor performance on them. Hence, further justifying that frequency should not be the only factor concerned when dealing with online multi-class imbalanced classification.

Moreover, other than classes being imbalanced, the class label for all instances might not be readily available, and there might be instances with missing labels. That is, labelling all instances in a stream in a timely manner may be impossible or prohibitively costly [65]. For instance, in our earlier example of intrusion detection, the label for all connections might not be available, or it might take some time for those labels to be available for training classifiers. However, due to the lack of data, training classifiers on scarce labelled data might significantly reduce the performance. For addressing this problem, semi-supervised learning (SSL) algorithms for data streams are being actively researched [79]. More specifically, these algorithms utilize both labelled and unlabelled instances for building more robust models.

For instance, online reliable semi-supervised learning (OReSSL) [63] and semi-supervised pool and accuracy-based stream classification (SPASC) [32] are two recent methods that rely on clustering or maintaining clusters of labelled and unlabelled data points. Some other online SSL algorithms rely on using the most confident predictions of models for labelling unlabelled instances (pseudo-labelling). For example, in streaming co-forest (SCo-Forest) [71], each classifier in the forest is trained using the most confident prediction of classifiers.

Current methods have the disadvantage of making only limited use of labelled data. Furthermore, by choosing incorrect instances, these methods have the ability to introduce false information, potentially leading to sub-optimal outcomes [65, 79]. These algorithms need to deal with this limitation by reducing the number of incorrect pseudo-labels.

1.2 Objective

Our first objective in this **book** is to address online multi-class im-balanced learning. That is, our purpose is to build methods that can maintain a balanced performance over all classes in the stream, even in the most skewed cases. We aim to achieve this by over-sampling instances in the minority classes, while under-sampling instances in the majority classes. In this way, our approaches would potentially have a better performance in the minority classes, which are often times more critical (recall the case with detecting the intrusion type).

For this purpose, we seek to propose techniques for dealing with on-line imbalanced learning that consider the frequency and performance of the classifier for each class. In this way, we only perform balancing when the performance of the classifier in a class is lower than the average performance over all classes, and hence, dealing with the problems associated with unnecessary samplings.

Furthermore, our second objective is to develop robust models that can achieve superior performance, even when labels are scarce. That is, we seek to develop models that can utilize both labelled and unlabelled instances in order to achieve better results than solely using labelled instances. More specifically, we aim to find accurate pseudo-labels, i.e., confident label predictions, for unlabelled instances that can effectively improve the performance of classifiers learning in such environments. Our goal is to limit the potential negative impact of introducing false information by incorporating a framework that can effectively select the most appropriate unlabelled instances for pseudo-labelling.

We summarize the contributions of this **book** below:
We introduce a novel approach for learning from multi-class imbalanced streams that involves balancing the training sets dynamically based on the current performance for each class. In the first variant, the Improved SMOTE Online Ensembles (ISOE), we employ Synthetic Minority Oversampling Technique (SMOTE), an effective over-sampling method, to over-sample the minority instances in the most recent window while dynamically re-sampling all classes based on individual recall rates. In the second variant, Improved Online Ensembles (IOE), we re-balance the classes' sample sizes by dynamically re-sampling based on each class's frequency and recall score. By re-sampling based on the recall score of classes, we balance the performance over all classes, and

hence, improving the overall results.

Furthermore, we propose a method for dealing with missing labels in data streams by using meta-learning and reinforcement learning. Meta-learning, or *learning how to learn*, is a sub-field in machine learning where a model is trained on source tasks in order to achieve generalization on new tasks [31], while reinforcement learning is another sub-field in machine learning aiming to train models by providing reward signals. We introduce the Online Reinforce SSL algorithm, which consists of a meta-reinforcement learning agent, various K nearest neighbours (K-NN) classifiers, and a base-learner. For each unlabelled instance, the agent chooses the prediction of one of the K-NN classifiers. Subsequently, the prediction is used as the pseudo-label for an incoming unlabelled instance, and the pseudo-labelled instance is utilized for training the base-learner. The meta-reinforcement learning agent is trained on various fully labelled datasets by extracting meta-features, and directly deployed to the target dataset for pseudo-labelling. We demonstrate that this algorithm accurately distinguishes between correct and incorrect predictions and show that our results outperform the current state-of-the-art.

The novelty of our approach is the use of a meta-RL model for pseudo-labelling unlabelled instances, which effectively reduces the amount of false pseudo-labels. To the best of our knowledge, this is the first time Reinforcement Learning has been used in the context of online semi-supervised learning, which is one of the main contributions of this **book**.

1.3 book **organization**

This **book** is organized as follow:

In chapter 2, we detail and review the background in relevant areas namely data streams, imbalanced learning, semi-supervised learning as well as reinforcement learning.

Chapter 3 introduces our improved online ensemble approach for dealing with imbalanced data. We illustrate the results of our proposed algorithm when compared to the state-of-the-art. We further introduce a method based on one nearest neighbours that effectively pseudo-labels unlabelled instances in an imbalanced data stream containing missing labels, thus addressing the combined problem of online multi-class imbalanced and semi-supervised learning.

In chapter 4, we further explore online semi-supervised learning by introducing our Online Reinforce methodology that employs meta-features to select the most appropriate instances for labeling. Our Online Reinforce algorithm includes a deep reinforcement Learning (DRL) agent that employs multiple k nearest neighbours classifiers to facilitate the online pseudo-labelling process. The chapter includes our detailed experimental comparison with the state-of-the-art.

Finally, in chapter 5, we conclude the **book**.

Chapter 2

Background

In this chapter, we first provide an overview of data streams and related topics. Next, we define imbalanced environments and methods for dealing with imbalanced datasets. Subsequently, we describe semi-supervised learning algorithms. Finally, the preliminaries of reinforcement learning are described as the last section of this chapter.

2.1   Data streams and online learning

Recall that data streams are large sequences of data, arriving online, either instance by instance, or in batches, that are possibly infinite and temporarily ordered [7, 22]. Due to the vast amounts of data, storing all the instances might be infeasible. Algorithms performing in these environments need to consider these characteristics. That is, online learning algorithms need to process each instance promptly and keep the memory bounded by learning instances incrementally [7, 20]. In this section, we first describe the classification task and present the classifiers utilized in this study. We also discuss techniques for evaluating the results of learning in data streaming environment. Subsequently, we turn our attention to evolving data.

2.1.1 Classifiers

We define classification in streams similar to [48]:

Given instances in a stream as $\{(x_1, y_1), ..., (x_t, y_t)\}$, where x_i is the feature vectors, and y_i is the label for instance at time i, the task of classifiers in the streaming environments is to incrementally update a classification function $f(x_i) \mapsto y_i$ such that a performance measure is maximized.

Now that we have defined classification in data streams, we move on to describing online classifiers. There are many classifiers introduced in the literature for data streams [7]. However, we only focus on the algorithms that are utilized in this study and are most commonly used because of their effectiveness.

Majority class

The majority class classifier is a baseline classifier that predicts the class with the most instances at each time step. That is, the number of instances for each class is updated and stored at each time step, and the class with the majority number of instances is selected for each arriving instance. This classifier does not consider the features associated with each instance. Due to only keeping the number of instances in each class and making predictions by comparing these numbers, the majority classifier can perform very quickly and on a limited memory. This classifier is only considered as a baseline and to determine how well an algorithm is performing when compared to a classifier predicting the most frequent class [7, 20].

No change classifier

The no change classifier is another baseline classifier that utilizes the class of the last previously seen instance as the prediction for a new instance [7]. That is, for an instance arriving at time t, the no change classifier utilizes the label for instance $t-1$ as the prediction for instance

t. Similar to the majority class classifier, this classifier acts as a baseline and needs very limited memory (the class label of the last instance), while performing quickly.

Algorithm 1 Hoeffding Tree classifier [7]

1: **function** HOEFFDING TREE(*Stream*)
2:     **for** every instance (x,y) in *stream* **do**
3:         Sort (x,y) to leaf l
4:         update counts n
5:         **if** examples at l not from the same class **then**
6:             Compute G for each attribute
7:             **if** G(best attribute)-G(second best attribute) > Hoeffding bound 2.1
    then
8:                 Split leaf based on the best attribute
9:                 **for** Each branch **do**
10:                     Start and initialize new leaf
11:                 **end for**
12:             **end if**
13:         **end if**
14:     **end for**
15: **end function**

Hoeffding Tree classifier

The Hoeffding tree classifier (HT) [33] is a decision tree classifier suitable for streaming environments. In a HT, splits are computed after sufficient instances arrive in the stream. In this way, instances are not reused, and the tree requires less memory. The splitting of HT is based on the Hoeffding bound [7, 33]:

$$\epsilon = \sqrt{\frac{R^2 \ln 1/\delta}{2n}}, \tag{2.1}$$

where δ is the desired confidence level, R is the range of the random variable, and n is the number of values collected [7]. That is, the information gain for attributes is collected, and if the difference between the attributes with the highest and the second-highest information gain is higher than ϵ, then the tree is split based on the attribute with the highest information gain. Due to the characteristics mentioned, HTs can perform very fast while needing limited memory [22].

Naïve Bayes

Naïve Bayes is a classifier that is naturally incremental [22], and uses the Bayes theorem for computing the probability for each class. That is, for predicting each instance, the probability for each class is computed, and the class with the highest probability is selected as the prediction for the instance [7]. The probability that an instance x is in class c is calculated by the equation below:

$$P(c|x) = \frac{P(x|c).P(c)}{P(x)} \tag{2.2}$$

where $P(c|x)$ is the posterior probability, and $P(x|c)$ is the prior probability. After computing this probability for each class, the class with the highest probability is selected as the prediction for each instance arriving from the stream. Since instances are not stored, and the probabilities of classes are updated incrementally, this algorithm requires limited memory.

K Nearest Neighbours

The K-NN classifier is a lazy algorithm that looks for the K nearest neighbours of an instance. Subsequently, the most common label of the K nearest neighbours is selected as the prediction for new testing instances [7, 18]. The closest neighbours are computed by calculating, e.g., the Euclidean distance between the instances. In online learning, a sliding window of size w is used for selecting the nearest neighbours in data streams. That is, the w most recent instances are considered for computing the nearest neighbours. As the size of w increases, the memory and the time complexity of the K-NN algorithm also increases.

OzaBag

The OzaBag classifier [17] is the online version of the bagging classifier.

Bagging classifiers are ensemble methods that sample instances from the dataset with replacement for training the base classifiers in the ensemble [9]. The OzaBag classifier consists of M base-learners, each of which is trained independently. Instead of sampling with replacement, as in the original Bagging algorithm, the online algorithm uses the Poisson distribution. That is, for each instance in the data stream, each base-learner in M is trained k times, where k is obtained from the equation below [17]:

$$P(K = k) \sim Poisson(1) = \frac{e^{-1}}{k!} \qquad (2.3)$$

After all M classifiers are trained, the algorithm moves on to the next instance in the stream. Uniform voting over the M base-learners is used for prediction in testing instance [22]. The choice of the base-learner impacts the memory and time complexity of this algorithm.

OzaBoost

The OzaBoost classifier is another algorithm introduced by [17], which is the online version of the Ada-Boost classifier [21]. The Ada-Boost algorithm works by adjusting the weight to the instances that are mis classified by the algorithm, which results in more focus on these instances. In the online version of this algorithm, the weights are set by setting the λ parameter in the Poisson distribution. The OzaBoost algorithm includes m base learners $\{h_1, ..., h_M\}$ which are trained sequentially. Similar to the OzaBag classifier, each base-learner is trained k times, where k is obtained from the equation below:

$$P(K = k) \sim Poisson(\lambda) = \frac{\lambda^k e^{-\lambda}}{k!} \qquad (2.4)$$

When an instance (x_i, y_i) arrives from the stream, λ is set to 1, and the first classifier h_1 is trained on (x_i, y_i) k times. Subsequently, h_1 is used for predicting the same instance (x_i, y_i). If the prediction of h_1 is the same as y_i, then λ for the next classifier is decreased. Similarly, if the prediction of h_1 is not the same as y_i, then the λ for the next classifier is increased. In this way, each base-learner in the ensemble is focused on specific examples. Based on [7], OzaBoost might be more sensitive to noises when compared to the OzaBag classifier.

The reader is reminded, as already noted above, that there are numerous other algorithms introduced in the online learning literature, such as [36, 50, 68]. However, we limit the overview of the online learning algorithms to the methods used in this study. In the next section, we describe how these techniques may be evaluated in the streaming environments.

2.1.2 Evaluation

In traditional machine learning, datasets are split into a training and a testing set, where training sets are used for training models, while testing sets are utilized to evaluate the model's performance on new unseen data points. K-fold Cross-validation is another method for evaluating models in traditional machine learning, where data is separated into K folds, one fold for testing while the remaining $k - 1$ folds are used for training the model; this procedure is applied k times, and the model is evaluated on all k folds [35]. In data streams, however, due to having unlimited instances, splitting the data into training and testing sets becomes challenging [22, 23]. That is, as infinite instances might arrive from the stream, separating train and test data might be more challenging than fixed-sized datasets in traditional machine learning. Furthermore, in streaming environments, evaluation methods need to show and consider the average performance over the stream [7]. Two approaches are introduced for evaluating classifiers in data streams, namely prequential test-than-train and holdout evaluation [22]. Prequential test-than-train uses each instance as both training and testing data point, while holdout evaluation holds a batch of data points at each k instance for evaluation purposes. We describe both of these methods in more details:

In **Prequential test-than-train**, each instance is used both for training and testing. As each instance arrives, the classifier predicts the label for the instance, and the prediction is compared to the true label for that instance. Subsequently, the instance is then used for training the classifier. In this way, the classifier is both tested and trained over all the instances [22, 23]. Moreover, we can compute the average performance of the model as instances arrive from the stream. Figure 2.1 illustrates the flow-chart of the prequential test-than-train evaluation method.

In **Holdout evaluation**, a separate batch of data is held out for testing purposes. The testing takes place periodically after k instances are seen [7, 23]. Unlike prequential test-than-train, this method does not train the classifier on all the data.

Evaluation metrics

Numerous evaluation metrics may be used in streaming environments, and the choice of the most appropriate evaluation metrics strongly depends on the characteristics of the data. Below we describe two of the most used evaluation metrics in the literature which are employed in this study.

Accuracy

In this method, the number of correct predictions is divided by the number of total instances. In prequential test-than-train, the accuracy is updated as each instance arrives, while in holdout evaluation, the accuracy is updated based on each batch of testing data. The accuracy

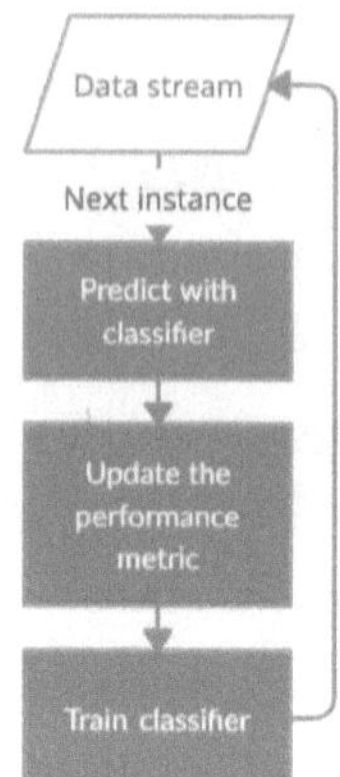

Figure 2.1: Flow chart of the prequential test-than-train evaluation method.

is obtained from the equation below:

$$Accuracy = \frac{correct\ predictions}{all\ predictions} \qquad (2.5)$$

κ scores

In some cases, such as in imbalanced domains, accuracy might not provide satisfactory evaluation over the models [7]. That is, the accuracy might be biased towards classes with higher number of instances. Moreover, accuracy does not consider the temporal dependence of instances in the stream. To this end, the κ statistics were introduced by [13], which evaluate the performance of a model by comparing it to a classifier that predicts instances randomly. Given the prequential accuracy of a classifier as p_0, and the probability that a random classifier would correctly classify an instance as p_c, the κ score would be estimated based on equation below [7].

$$\kappa = \frac{p_0 - p_c}{1 - P_c} \qquad (2.6)$$

A κ score of 1 suggests that the classifier is always correct, and a κ score of 0 means that the classifier correctly predicts instances as often as a classifier with a random chance. The κ statistic can also be modified by including the majority classifier or the no-change classifier instead of the random classifier [7]. For instance, by using the no-change classifier, the κ evaluation metric can address the temporal dependence between instances of the stream [10]. Furthermore, κ statistics may be computed very efficiently, making them an effective evaluation metric in streaming environments [24].

In the following sub-section, we provide an overview of concept drifts, which are one of the main challenges in learning from streams, and take place when the distribution of the data evolves.

2.1.3 Concept drifts

Recall that concept drifts occur when there is a change in the distribution of the data. Streams that contain drifts in their distribution are called *non-stationary* or *evolving* streams [7]. In contrast, *stationary* streams are defined as streams that do not contain concept drifts, and the distribution of the data does not change during the stream.

Algorithms learning in non-stationary streams need to maintain their model performance throughout the data. That is, techniques need to deal with changes in the distribution of data by potentially "forgetting" the past knowledge and focusing on the newer concepts [7, 61]. Concept drift detectors are used as methods for detecting these changes in the distribution of the data [20].

In general, concept drifts can be categorized into four (4) classes, namely gradual, incremental, sudden, and recurrent [7, 61].

Abrupt changes

Abrupt changes happen when the distribution of the data changes

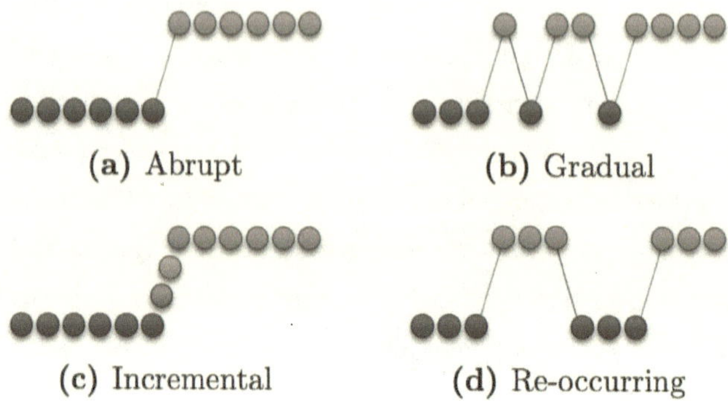

Figure 2.2: Types of drift [18]

rapidly [62]. These changes happen suddenly in very few time steps, meaning that the distribution of the data changes to a new distribution suddenly. In these changes, models need to adapt by forgetting the previous knowledge and learning the new concept.

Gradual changes

Unlike abrupt drifts, gradual changes do not happen suddenly. In these changes, the distribution changes slowly, while having examples from both distributions until the data shifts to the new distribution completely [18]. Figure 2.2 (b) demonstrates how gradual drifts take place in a stream.

Incremental changes

Incremental changes happen slowly over longer time steps. In these changes, the difference in the distribution is barely visible when looked at over few time steps[7, 62]; however, when this change is accumulated, the change in the distribution of the data becomes significant.

Recurrent or re-occurring changes

Recurrent changes are changes that take place multiple times throughout the stream. In other words, the distribution of the data might revert back to a previously seen distribution [61]. An example of these changes can be found in seasonal datasets [7]. For instance, when the season changes from summer to winter and from winter to summer, the distribution of data reverts back to a previously seen concept.

2.1.4 Drift detection

Drift detection methods use the statistics gathered directly from the incoming data or the performance of the classifier. Gama et. al. formalises three requirements for concept drift detectors [61]. Firstly, the concept drift detectors need to detect concepts with minimal delay. Secondly, concept drift detectors need to be able to distinguish from the actual drift and natural noise in the data. Finally, concept drift detectors need to meet the previous requirements while using limited memory and time. Drift detectors need to meet these requirements for effectively detecting concept drifts. According to [11], drift detectors are evaluated based on true and false detection rates, missing drifts, and delays in detection. Other than detecting drift, some drift detection methods provide a warning signal which suggests that the distribution of the data might be changing [1, 26]. If this change is persistent, then the drift detector detects concept drift in the stream. Below we detail some of the widely used drift detectors. There are many drift detection methods introduced in the literature, but we only focus on the methods that are utilized in this study, and are widely used in the literature because of their effectiveness.

DDM

Drift Detection Method (DDM) is a drift detection method introduced in [26], which consider the number of errors of the classifier for detecting drifts. That is, DDM calculates two thresholds based on the minimum and standard deviation of the error rates on time t, one associated with the warning signal and the other for the drift signal. If the error rate reaches any of these thresholds, the appropriate signal is then declared by DDM. However, DDM might not be able to detect abrupt drifts fast enough [4]. Due to this limitation, EDDM was proposed to detect more sudden drifts in the data, as described next.

EDDM

Early Drift Detection Method (EDDM) [4] is an extension of the DDM method. In this method, the average distance between miss classifications is computed rather than the error rates used in the DDM method. Similar to DDM, two thresholds are used for the warning signal and the drift signal. When the distance at time t divided by max distance reaches any of the thresholds, the signal associated with the threshold is declared by EDDM. This method can be very effective when there are abrupt drifts in the data, but could also result in false detections, as shown in our experiments in chapter 4.

ADWIN

Adaptive windowing (ADWIN) [6] is another drift detection method that uses a window over bits or numbers. While concept drift is not detected, the size of the window increases as the instances arrive. When concept drift is detected, the size of the window shrinks. ADWIN detects concepts in the data by dividing the window into two separate windows w_0 and w_1, and checks if w_0 and w_1 are generated from the same distribution. One of the significant advantages of this method is that, unlike other methods such as DDM and EDDM, there is no need to set a value for the size of the window.

FHDDM and FHDDMS

Fast Hoeffding Drift Detection Method (FHDDM) is a drift detection method introduced in [18, 49]. In this method, if the difference between the mean of the current window and the maximum mean is greater

Algorithm 2 FHDDM [48, 49]

1: Initialize window w
2: $\mu^m = 0$
3: **function** DETECT DRIFT($instance$)
4:     update counts n
5:     **if** w.size $= $ n **then**
6:         w.tail.drop()
7:     **else**
        return False
8:     **end if**
9:     w.puch($instace$)
10:     $\mu^t = \frac{w.count(1)}{w.size()}$
11:     **if** $\mu^t > \mu^m$ **then**
12:         $\mu^m = \mu^t$
13:     **end if**
14:     **if** $(\mu^m - \mu^t) >= $ Hoeffding bound 2.1 **then**
        return True
15:     **else**
        return False
16:     **end if**
17: **end function**

than the Hoeffding inequality, drift is detected. In the second variation of this algorithm, FHDDMS, the authors use two sliding windows for detecting concept drifts. In FHDDMS, a short sliding window is used for detecting abrupt drifts, while a longer sliding window is used for detecting the number of false positives caused by the shorter sliding window. Both FHDDM and FHDDMS are very fast drift detectors. However, unlike the ADWIN method, the sliding-window sizes need to be specified as a hyperparameter.

We detailed online learning and the challenges associated with learning in streaming environments. In the next section, we describe imbalanced learning, and the problems of learning in such environments.

2.2　Imbalanced learning

Recall that imbalanced learning is one of the major challenges in machine learning. Imbalanced learning is defined as having an unequal distribution of classes, where the difference between the distributions is significant [30]. In such cases, the classes with the least number of instances become unrepresented in the dataset [17]. Applications of imbalanced learning may be found in areas such as machinery fault diagnosis, where the number of instances in the negative class is more significant than the number of instances in the positive class [28].

Recall that in imbalanced binary classification, the class with fewer instances is called a minority class, while the class with the most instances is called the majority class. On the other hand, in multi-class imbalanced learning, there might be multiple minority and majority classes represented in the dataset.

A main challenge in learning from imbalanced datasets is that the classifier might be biased towards the majority classes [17]. That is, when the distribution of the classes is not equal, the classifier focuses all attention on learning the majority class. This could significantly reduce the classifying performance of the classifier in the minority classes, which may be more critical than the majority classes, e.g., when attempting to detect rare concepts. For instance, consider a three-class scenario where 95% of the instances belong to the majority class, while the minority class instances are 3% and 2%, respectively. A highly biased classifier may yield an accuracy of 95%, while mis-classifying all the minority instances.

Furthermore, the evaluation of classifiers in imbalanced datasets should contain the classifier's performance on both minority and majority classes, individually. In imbalanced datasets, using methods such as accuracies should not be considered for evaluating a model's performance [28]. For instance, let us say that in a multi-class dataset, 90% of the data consists of the majority class, while the other 10% is distributed between the two minority classes. In this dataset, a classifier only predicting the majority class will have an accuracy of 90%. This implies that in cases of imbalanced dataset, other metrics are needed for evaluating the performance of classifiers [17, 69].

During learning, it follows that classifiers ideally need to maintain high performance over all the classes, and notably produce high quality models against the minorities. To this end, imbalanced learning methods are introduced for training classifiers to have balanced performance over minority and majority classes. In the book "Learning from imbalanced data sets", the authors categorize these methods into four classes: algorithm level, data level, cost-sensitive, and ensemble methods [17]. Algorithm level methods deal with this problem by modifying the classifier to focus on the minority classes [27]. The data level approaches or sampling methods create instances from minority classes [12], or remove instances from majority classes to make the dataset balanced [38], while cost-sensitive methods increase the weight of instances in the minority classes or increase the cost of miss-classification of these instances. Finally, ensemble-based methods combine sampling methods and cost-sensitive methods to train multiple base-classifiers that are biased towards the minority classes [17, 59]. Below we describe more sampling methods (data level) approaches used in the literature and in this book.

2.2.1 Sampling methods

Recall that sampling methods are generally categorized into three classes, namely oversampling, under-sampling, and hybrid methods containing a mix of both. Oversampling methods either duplicate instances or create synthetic instances, while under-sampling techniques remove majority instances from the dataset. There are many variants of sampling methods introduced for dealing with class imbalanced. In this section, we only cover the sampling methods that are used in this **book**.

Random under-sampling

Random under-sampling, as the name suggests, randomly removes instances from the majority classes. Consequently, all the classes would have the same number of instances as the minority class [28], thus potentially discarding important regions of information from the dataset [37].

Random oversampling

Random oversampling, on the other hand, randomly duplicates minority class instances. In this approach, instances in the minority classes are duplicated until all the classes have the same number of instances as the majority class, which implies that one may overfit the model by duplicating instances [11, 37].

Algorithm 3 SMOTE [12]

```
1: function SMOTE(data,k)
2:     for instance in data do
3:         if instance is minority then
4:             neighbours = computeKneighbours(instance)    ▷ K nearest neighbours
5:             random_neighbour = rand.int(0,k)              ▷ Select one neighbour
6:             neighbour = neighbours [random_neighbour]
7:             for att in all attributes do
8:                 diff = neighbour.att - instance.att        ▷ Calculate the difference
9:                 gap = rand(0,1)
10:                synthetic.att = instance.att + diff*gap
11:            end for
12:            add synthetic insance to the data
13:        end if
14:    end for
15: end function
```

SMOTE

Synthetic Minority Oversampling Technique (SMOTE) [12] is an effective oversampling method that creates synthetic instances for the minority classes. More specifically, k nearest neighbours for each minority instance is computed. Subsequently, one of the k neighbours is selected. A new synthetic instance for the minority class is created by computing the difference between the feature space of the two neighbours, while adding random noise. Algorithm 3 describes the above steps in more details.

SCUT

In cases of extreme multi-class imbalanced datasets, oversampling can lead to creating many synthetic instances for the minority classes, while under-sampling can lead to losing significant data points from the majority classes. SMOTE and Clustered Undersampling Technique (SCUT) is an algorithm developed by [1], that uses both oversampling and under-sampling. In this method, minority classes are oversampled based on the SMOTE algorithm, while the majority classes are under-sampled based on clusters of the data.

The described sampling methods are utilized in the literature and this study because of their effectiveness and performance. In the next section, we detail how these algorithms may be evaluated in imbalanced learning environments.

2.2.2 Evaluation

Recall that the accuracy evaluation metric is often biased towards the majority class, and should not be considered in imbalanced datasets. Evaluation metrics used in imbalanced learning need to consider the performance over minority and majority classes individually [17].

Suppose we have a binary classification with positive and negative classes. True positives (TP) and true negatives (TN) are instances in the positive class and negative class that are correctly classified. False positives (FP) and false negatives (FN), on the other hand, are instances that are not correctly classified. That is FP are instances that are falsely classified as positive, while FN are instances that are falsely classified as negative. Sensitivity or recall score is defined as:

$$recall = \frac{TP}{TP + FN} \tag{2.7}$$

With recall scores, we can understand how many of the positive instances are correctly classified. Precision score on the other hand is defined as:

$$precision = \frac{TP}{TP + FP} \tag{2.8}$$

With precision scores, we can determine how many of the instances classified as positive are correctly classified. Some performance measures such as F-measures and Geometric mean (G-means) combine these metrics into a single metric [17]. Given the precision and recall for the positive class, F-measure can be defined as below:

$$F - measure = 2 * \frac{precision.recall}{precision + recall} \tag{2.9}$$

However, the F-measure does not consider the performance of the classifier for the negative class [8]. G-means is another method that considers the individual score of both positive and negative classes, which is defined as below:

$$G - means = \sqrt{\frac{TP}{TP + FN} \cdot \frac{TN}{TN + FP}} \tag{2.10}$$

In order to obtain higher scores for G-means, a classifier must maintain a balanced performance over both minority and majority class. However, when there are more than two classes involved, the G-means score may be extended to include all the classes based on the equation below, which can also be described as the "geometric average of the recall scores" [8]:

$$G - means = \sqrt[|C|]{\prod_{c \in C} recall_c}, \tag{2.11}$$

where C is all the classes in a dataset, and $recall_c$ is the recall score for class c. With this method, we are able to evaluate the performance of a classifier in a multi-class class imbalanced with multiple minority and majority classes. Having lower values of G-means would suggest that the classifier is not maintaining the performance over all classes, whereas having a higher G-means indicates that the classifier is keeping a balanced performance across all classes. As a result, in this **book**, G-means is the primary method for evaluating the performance of classifiers in multi-class class imbalanced datasets. The G-means metric may also be calculated online by estimating the recall score for each class in an online manner.

We described imbalanced learning as well as sampling methods for dealing with challenges involved in learning from imbalanced data. In the next section, we introduce semi-supervised learning.

2.3 Semi-supervised learning

Recall that semi-supervised learning is a sub-field of machine learning aimed at creating accurate models when not all labels are immediately available [65]. That is, semi-supervised learning algorithms feature improved performances due to training based on a small set of labelled instances, combined with a large number of unlabelled instances [79].

In general, semi-supervised classification may be categorized into two settings, namely inductive and transductive techniques [65, 79]. Given labelled data points (x_l, y_l), and unlabelled data points (x_u), the goal of inductive SSL methods is to yield a predictive model for predicting labels for (x_u), and unseen data points beyond (x_u). Transductive methods, on the other hand, do not train a model for predicting instances. In transductive methods, given the labelled data (x_l, y_l), and unlabelled data points (x_u), the goal is to find the labels for unlabelled instances (x_u) directly, and unlike inductive methods, transductive methods are not required to perform on unseen instances [79].

2.3.1   Wrapper methods

Wrapper-based methods are inductive methods for dealing with missing labels. These methods work by training a classifier (or multiple classifiers), and using the predictions of the classifier for pseudo-labelling unlabelled instances. The pseudo-labelled instances are then used as training data for the classifier. Below we discuss three wrapper methods, namely self-training, co-training, and tri-training.

Self-training

Self-training is a wrapper method that uses the most confident predictions of the classifier. That is, for each unlabelled instance, the confidence probability and the prediction are estimated. If the confidence of probability for the unlabelled instances is higher than a pre-defined threshold, then the prediction is used as the label for the unlabelled instance. Consequently, the classifier is trained on the pseudo-labelled instance.

Co-training

Co-training is another wrapper-based technique where two or more classifiers are used for prediction. At each iteration, the most confident predictions of a classifier are used for training the other classifiers in the co-training framework. Furthermore, each classifier is provided with a separate view of the data, each view being a separate subset of the feature space [65]. Consequently, multiple views of the data are considered for prediction, and hence, the model can better use the unlabelled instances for training.

Tri-training

Tri-training [78] is another wrapper method in which three classifiers are trained alternatively. In this method, two classifiers are used for predicting the unlabelled instance, and if the two classifiers agree, the prediction is used as the label for the third classifier.

Overall, wrapper methods are effective SSL methods that may be paired with most supervised learning algorithms. However, a drawback of these approaches is that they might introduce false information by adding incorrect instances to the training data [65, 79]

So far, in this chapter, we reviewed data streams and online learning, defined imbalanced learning and semi-supervised learning, and we detailed the challenges associated with each problem. In the next section we provide a brief overview of Reinforcement Learning, which is one of the main components of our proposed method in chapter 4.

2.4   Reinforcement learning

Reinforcement learning (RL) is a sub-field of machine learning and Artificial Intelligence (AI), where an agent learns by performing actions in an environment and receiving the reward for each action. In this type of learning, the agent learns the optimal behaviour by experiencing and exploring the environment. The agent in RL is defined as the decision-maker, while the environment is anything that the agent interacts with. Furthermore, the environment provides the agent rewards for each action taken. These rewards serve as the feedback for actions taken by the agent. In RL, the problem is to maximize the expected cumulative reward of the agent by using methods that incorporate trail-and-error searches [3]. This problem can be formulated as a Markov decision problem (MDP) [60]. At each time step, the agent receives a **state** S_t and takes an **action** A_t. The environment then provides the state S_{t+1}, and the **reward** R_{t+1}, which are the consequences of the action A_t [60]. Figure 2.3 demonstrates how the agent interacts with the environment. Hence, the goal of RL is to maximize the expected return at each time

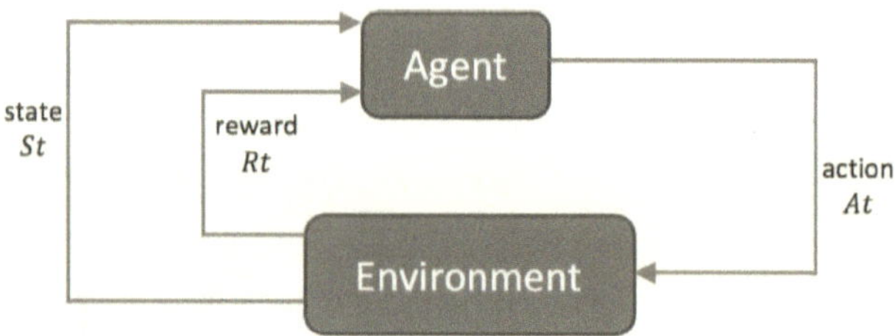

Figure 2.3: How an agent interacts with an environment [60].

step t based on the equation below:

$$G_t = \sum_{k=0}^{\infty} \gamma^k R_{t+k+1}, \tag{2.12}$$

where γ is the discount factor, and serves as the trade-off between the immediate and the future rewards. By lowering the value of γ, immediate rewards become more valuable.

A **policy** π is defined as the mapping between states and the probability of each action. The **value function** defines the value of each state in terms of future rewards, which under the policy π is defined as [60]:

$$V_\pi(s_t) = \mathbb{E}_\pi [G_t | s_t] \tag{2.13}$$

The value function may also be extended to include state-action pairs. That is, state-action pairs determine how valuable an action in a state is. Therefore, the value of taking action a_t in the state s_t under the policy π is defined as the **q-value** $q_\pi(a_t, s_t)$:

$$q_\pi(s_t, a_t) = \mathbb{E}_\pi[G_t \,|\, s_t, a_t] \tag{2.14}$$

Both value function and q-values are crucial components of most reinforcement learning methods [60]. These two equations can be further expanded using Bellman equations. By expanding equation 2.13, we have:

$$V_\pi(s_t) = \mathbb{E}_\pi[R_{t+1} + \gamma G_{t+1} \,|\, s_t] \tag{2.15}$$

By expanding based on possible state, rewards, and actions the equation 2.15 can be further expanded [60]:

$$V_\pi(s_t) = \sum_a \pi(a|s) \sum_{s',r} p(s',r|s,a)[r + \gamma \mathbb{E}_\pi[G_{t+1}|s_{t+1}]] \tag{2.16}$$

In this equation, the expected return $\mathbb{E}_\pi[G_{t+1}|s_{t+1}]$ is the same as equation 2.13 for the state s_{t+1}. Finally, by replacing the expected return with the $V(s_{t+1})$ we would have the Bellman equation for the state-value function [60]:

$$V_\pi(s_t) = \sum_a \pi(a|s) \sum_{s',r} p(s',r|s,a)[r + \gamma V_\pi(s_{t+1})] \tag{2.17}$$

Similarly, by performing the above steps for the q-values, we would have the Bellman equation for the action-value function [60]:

$$q_\pi(s_t, a_t) = \sum_{s',r} p(s',r|s,a)[r + \gamma \sum_{a'} \pi(a'|s)q_\pi(s_{t+1}, a')] \tag{2.18}$$

The Bellman equations above are the fundamentals of the RL algorithms. By using these equations, the value function for each state can be computed recursively as a function of the value of the successor states [60].

Moreover, these values may be stored in a tabular format by saving the value for each state or state-action pair in the memory. However, as the number of states increases, the amount of memory increases drastically. For instance, in continuous problems where states could have any number between 0 and 1, storing all the possible states is not feasible. These values may also be estimated by function approximates such as neural networks [60]. That is, a neural network with parameters θ is trained to estimate the value of states at a given time. Methods such as Deep Q-learning use a neural network for estimating Q functions. Other methods such as actor-critic, train an actor or policy for selecting actions, and a critic that estimates the value for states [55].

In chapter 4, we detail our Online Reinforce SSL methodology, which features an RL agent selecting the prediction of K-NN classifiers as pseudo-labels for unlabelled instances.

2.5 Summary

In this chapter, we reviewed the background concepts of data stream mining, imbalanced learning, and semi-supervised learning. Notably, in section 2.1, we described the preliminary of data streams and the challenges involved in learning from the streams,concept drifts and concept drift detectors for dealing with non-stationary data. In section 2.2, we explained imbalanced learning and sampling methods used for dealing with imbalanced data. In section 2.3, we provided details regarding semi-supervised learning by describing inductive wrapper methods for dealing with missing labels in a dataset. Finally, in section 2.4, we described the preliminaries of reinforcement learning, which is one of the main components of our Online Reinforce SSL framework.

In the next chapter, we introduce our methods for dealing with the challenges involving imbalanced data streams. Furthermore, in chapter 4, we describe the Online Reinforce algorithm for dealing with missing labels.

Chapter 3

Improved Online Ensembles for dealing with online imbalanced learning

In this chapter, we detail our improved online ensemble (IOE) algorithm for dealing with multi-class online imbalanced learning, that also includes an approach for dealing with missing labels in imbalanced data streams using the previously introduced one nearest neighbour (1-NN) classifier. We evaluate our proposed method in both static and non-stationary streaming environments. Parts of this chapter were presented in the International Conference of Data Mining Workshops (ICDMW 2020), in the paper titled "Multi-class imbalanced semi-supervised learning from streams through online ensembles" [64].

3.1   Introduction

Recall that multi-class imbalanced is defined as having less frequent instances in one or more minority classes, when compared to the other (majority) classes. In such environments, the learner becomes biased towards the classes with higher frequencies, thus potentially harming the overall accuracies of the resultant models.

For addressing this issue, in this chapter, we introduce a novel approach to learning from multi-class imbalanced streams with missing labels that involves balancing the training sets dynamically during training. In the first variant, the Improved SMOTE Online Ensembles (ISOE), we employ the previously introduced SMOTE algorithm to over-sample the minority instances in the most recent window, while dynamically re-sampling all classes based on individual recall rates. In the second variant, Improved Online Ensembles (IOE), we re-balance the classes' sample sizes by changing the rate parameter based on the current performance and the number of instances of each class seen so far.

In addition, we introduce a window-based SSL approach for data streams employing the one nearest neighbour algorithm for labelling unlabelled instances. In this method, labels are only added if the distance between neighbours is closer than a threshold ϵ.

This chapter is organized as follows. Section 3.2 continues the background for imbalanced learning by extending it to data streams and online learning. In Section 3.3, a description of our online ensemble methodology is provided. Section 3.4 details our experimental evaluation, results and discussion.

3.2 Background and related work

3.2.1 Online imbalanced learning

In chapter 2, we detailed sampling methods for dealing with imbalanced learning datasets. However, in data streams, the sampling of classes needs to be performed in an online manner. For this reason, online imbalanced learning methods are being actively researched and we briefly discuss them here. For instance, Learn++.CDS is an ensemble-based model combining SMOTE and Learn++.NSE [14]. The Learn++.NSE component is used for dealing with concept drifts, while SMOTE is used for balancing the classes. Learn++.CDS updates the weights for classifiers based on their error rates for batches of data. However, the authors focused on binary classes only and did not consider environments with multiple classes. In addition, [42] introduced a voting-based weighted online sequential extreme learning machine (VWOS-ELM) algorithm for learning in imbalanced streams. However, a drawback of this method is that the class imbalance must be fixed and known in advance.

Recall that SCUT-DS [46] is an online multi-class learning algorithm that extends the SCUT [1] approach to the incremental learning setting. SCUT-DS uses a fixed window size of n to sample instances. When the window is full, the algorithm first uses the samples to test the classifier's performance, then uses sampling to balance the classes' distribution. The majority classes are under-sampled based on cluster centroids obtained via online k-means. The minority classes are over-sampled based on SMOTE. A drawback of this method is that only static data sets, i.e., streams that do not contain concept drifts, are considered.

In another work, [71] introduced resampling ensembles for binary class online learning in which over-sampling online bagging (OOB) is used to over-sample the minority classes by changing the rate parameter of the Poisson distribution in online bagging to W_{maj}/W_{min}, where W_{maj} is the number of samples taken from the majority class, and W_{min} is the number of samples taken from the minority class. Under-sampling online bagging (UOB), on the other hand, under-samples the majority class by changing the rate parameter of the Poisson distribution to W_{min}/W_{maj}. To focus on more recent samples, the authors further introduce a time-decaying factor that will allow the ensemble to forget the older data. They tested UOB and OOB on dynamic data streams that could undergo changes in the distributions of the classes and concluded that overall, UOB performs better on static data sets, while OOB is more robust to changes in the distribution of the classes. The authors extended their work to the multi-class scenario, with the aptly named MUOB and MOOB [73]. For MUOB, the rate parameter is set based on $min(w)/w_k$, while, for MOOB, the rate parameter is based on $max(w)/w_k$. Experimental evaluations confirmed that MOOB performs better in terms of G-means and stability when compared to MOUB and VWOS-ELM; this fact will also be confirmed in our experimental evaluation. Next, we focus our attention on concept drift detection algorithms for imbalanced streams.

3.2.2   Concept drifts for online imbalanced learning

Recall that concept drifts are very common in data streams and occur when the distribution of the data changes in such a way that the performance of the model decreases. As noted in chapter 2, a large number of algorithms exist, notably the error-based drift detection approaches, that track the performance and the error rate of the classifier in detecting drifts [10].

DDM-OCI is a recent extension of DDM that is used for concept drift detection in imbalanced datasets, and we use it in our work [70, 72]. The main difference between DDM-OCI and DDM is that, instead of tracking the error rates, DDM-OCI monitors the recalls on the minority class for detecting drifts. In order to focus on the more recent instances, the authors use a forgetting factor to focus on the changes in recent instances.

3.2.3 Online semi-supervised learning

Online semi-supervised learning from streams is an emerging area of research aimed at improving model results in data streams with scarce labelled data. Approaches used for dealing with online semi-supervised learning are based on wrapper methods, active-learning, and clustering methods [16, 29, 32, 63].

For instance, SAND (Semi-Supervised Adaptive Novel Class Detection and Classification over Data Stream) is an active semi-supervised ensemble method [29] developed for streams. In order to detect concepts, SAND estimates confidence scores. If the confidence scores decrease over time, the concept drift detector detects a change; hence, a new model will be trained on the new data. Samples with confidence scores higher than a threshold are used directly for training. The method seeks the labels of instances with confidence scores lower than the threshold from an oracle, and the model will be trained only after drift is detected. Once trained, the new model will replace the old model in the ensemble. However, in a streaming setting, asking an oracle for labels might not be feasible and could end up being very expensive.

LESS-TWE [19] is another online learning algorithm for semi-supervised learning environments. The algorithm monitors the distribution of the confidence scores for concept drifts. If the distribution of the confidence scores changes, then the model trains a new classifier based on new data. If an instance arrives without a label, the ensemble predicts a label for this instance. A major limitation of this approach is that it could emphasize false behaviour [65, 79].

Next, we detail our algorithms for online ensemble learning from multi-class imbalanced data streams in the presence of concept drifts and unlabelled data.

3.3 Methodology

3.3.1 Multi-class imbalanced learning

As noted above, our methodology combines ensembles and sampling based on instance frequencies and recall rates.

Recall that the Improved SMOTE Online Ensemble (ISOE) variant incorporates SMOTE for over-sampling minority classes into an online ensemble, while the sampling is done in conjunction with instance weight adaptations based on class recall rates. Specifically, our ISOE algorithm uses a sliding-window of size s for processing the data instances, where s is set by inspection. Let r_c and w_c be the recall score and size of class c, respectively. At the beginning of each window, both r_c and w_c will be updated incrementally based on [69].

$$w_c^t = \alpha * w_c^{(t-1)} + (1 - \alpha) * w_c^t \tag{3.1}$$

$$r_c^t = \alpha * r_c^{(t-1)} + (1 - \alpha) * r_c^t \tag{3.2}$$

In the equations above, t is the current window number, and c is the class number. Each window is over-sampled based on the SMOTE algorithm, and, after resampling, the online ensemble will be trained using the sampled data points. Similar to the OzaBag classifier, we use the Poisson distribution for training each base-learner in the ensemble [17]. Inspired by [71], we change the rate parameter for the Poisson distribution of the online ensemble according to the performance for each class. The rate parameter is set based on the recalls of the classes. If the absolute difference between the recall score for a class and the mean recall is higher than the pre-defined threshold, then the samples for this class will be sampled using the set parameter r.

$$k = Poisson(r_{avg-excluding-c}/r_c) \tag{3.3}$$

Here, r_c is the recall for class c, which is calculated based on Equation 3.3, and $r_{avg-excluding-c}$ is the average recall for the classes excluding class c. Using this approach, the recalls for all of the classes are balanced. If the recall for a class is higher than the average recall, then the class will be under-sampled and vice versa. Hence, the overall performance of the classifier should improve.

To emphasize the classes with lower recalls, the weights for the samples are set according to the previous rate parameter. Thus, there is greater focus on the classes with lower recall scores, and less attention is paid to the classes with high recall scores.

In the second variant of our algorithm (IOE), we eliminate SMOTE and only adjust the rate parameter as we sample instance by instance. Since no other sampling algorithm is used, IOE over-samples the minority classes by adding w to (3.3) [73]. If both r_c and w_c for class c are lower than the average r and the average w, respectively, class c is considered a minority class, and the rate parameter for this class is set based on:

$$k = Poisson((r_{avg-excluding-c}/r_c) * (max(W)/W_c)) \qquad (3.4)$$

where $max(w)$ is the maximum w for all the classes. By adding the second portion to the equation, the classes are balanced based on both performance and size. For classes other than those in the minority, the rate parameters is set based on (3.3). If $max(w)$ is significantly larger than w_c, k would have a large value, which could overfit the model. To address this issue, we set a max-value for k. If k is higher than the max-value, we set k equal to the max-value, which will then also be used as the weight of the instance for training.

Algorithm 4 describes how the rate parameters are set while considering each situation for both ISOE and IOE. In summary, as explained above, the main difference between IOE and ISOE is that ISOE uses

SMOTE for balancing the classes, while IOE relies on changing k only. Furthermore, ISOE uses a sliding window, while IOE processes the data instance by instance. Next, we will discuss the concept drift detection portion of our model.

3.3.2 Concept drift

In our work, we extend the previously introduced DDM-OCI algorithm [72] to multi-class environments. To this end, we track the recalls for each of the minority classes. DDM-OCI uses equation 3.2 to calculate the recalls for the classes. After drift is detected, the model is reset and trained based on the data received between the drift warning and detection. Moreover, we use another method similar to DDM-OCI that tracks the predictions on the minority classes instead of recalls. The drawback of both of these approaches is that the ground truths for all the instances may be needed, rendering them inapplicable to semi-supervised environments. In order to deal with this problem, we use an approach similar to those used in [29] and [19]. At each time step, the confidence scores for the classes are calculated. Following [19], we use a modified, unsupervised version of FHDDM to assess the confidence scores for the minority classes to watch for concept drifts. If there is a change in the distribution of the confidence scores, there will be a flag for drift in the data, and a new model will be trained based on new data. One of the benefits of this approach is that by using just the confidence scores, no ground truths are required for the labels.

3.3.3 Semi-supervised online learning with one nearest neighbours

Let $\{x1, x2, x3, ..., x_n\}$ be the set of samples in the data stream and $\{y1, y2, y3, ..., y_n\}$ be the labels associated with each of the samples. If some of these labels equal ϕ, then the samples associated with them cannot be used for training purposes. Recall that self-training is one of the methods used in semi-supervised environments to label unlabelled samples with classifiers' predictions [79]. In our methodology, we incorporated two methods:

Algorithm 4 ISOE/IOE

 1: **for** i, i= 1,2, ..., n **do**
 2:     X,y = window[i]
 3:     predictions = model.predict(X)
 4:     Recalls = update_recalls(predictions,y)
 5:     w = update_w(y)
 6:     **if** model == ISOE **then**
 7:        X, Y = SMOTE(X,Y)
 8:        model.fit(X, Y, Recalls,w)
 9:     **end if**
10: **end for**
11: **function** MODEL.FIT(X, y, $Recalls$,w)
12:     avg_recalls = AVG(Recalls)
13:     avg_w = AVG(w)
14:     **for** i, in Classes **do**
15:        **if** abs(Recalls[i]-avg_recalls) > threshold **then**
16:           **if** model == IOE and Recalls[i] < avg_recalls and W[i] < avg_w **then**
17:              weight[i],l[i] = (AVG(Recalls_exclude_i)/Recalls[i]) * (Max(w)/w[i])
18:           **else**
19:              weight[i],l[i] = (AVG(Recalls_exclude_i)/ Recalls[i])
20:           **end if**
21:           **if** l[i] > max_value **then**
22:              weight[i],l[i] = max_value
23:           **end if**
24:        **else**
25:           weight[i],l[i] = 1
26:        **end if**
27:     **end for**
28:     **for** i, in len(X) **do**
29:        k = Poisson(l[y[i]])
30:        **for** i, i =1,2,...,k **do**
31:           model.partial_fit(X[i],y[i],weight[y[i]])
32:        **end for**
33:     **end for**
34: **end function**

1- Using the most confident predictions of the main model (self-training).
2- Using a separate one nearest neighbor (1-NN) model.
Recall that one problem that emerges when using the model's predictions is that we might enforce the classifier's false behaviour by introducing false information [19, 65].

The assumption behind 1-NN is that closest neighbours would likely have the same labels [39]. However, the distance between the neighbours could be very far, which could reduce the likelihood of neighbours having the same label. To address this possibility, we consider only samples with distances between them, and their nearest neighbors, that are lower than a threshold ϵ. By using this approach, we assume that two neighbours would have the same label, if the distance between them is close enough. Limitations of our method is that it is highly dependent on the value of ϵ and the inherent assumption, of 1-NN, that the closest neighbors have the same labels. It follows that the idea may also be extended to include multiple neighbours (e.g. 3-NN, 5-NN). In such an extension, we would calculate the mean distance and choose the majority class from those instances that are closer than ϵ.

There are some additional challenges associated with using this approach for online learning. Due to limited memory, storing all the unlabelled and labelled samples is not possible. Also, iterating the samples more than once increases the time complexity of the algorithm. To alleviate these problems, we propose a method based on sliding windows to store both labelled and unlabelled instances. The full algorithm used to carry out the online 1-NN technique is described next. At each window, labelled samples are added to a window called labelled-window. The unlabelled samples are saved in the unlabelled-window. After the sizes of the unlabelled-window and labelled-window reach a pre-defined threshold (window-size), the get_label function is called.

Using the get_label function, the 1-NNs of all the unlabelled samples are computed. If the distance between an unlabelled sample and its nearest neighbor is less than ϵ, then the sample is labelled according to its neighbor. Otherwise, the unlabelled instance is discarded. Once completed, the labelled samples are added to the training set and both windows are emptied, as depicted in Algorithm 5. Note that ϵ is not a general hyperparameter since it can be different for each dataset. To obtain an approximation for the value of ϵ, we use the k quantile of the distances measured during the warm-up period. However, the best value for ϵ depends entirely on the data. If the data is normalized between 0 and 1, then ϵ should be set at a lower value. Note that, in our experimental evaluation, we will compare the results of these two semi-supervised learning methods.

3.4 Experimental evaluation

This section describes our experimental setup and details our datasets. Note that we used synthetic and real-world datasets that are widely used by the online learning community. Table 3.1 summarizes the datasets and includes the number of instances, number of classes and the percentage of each class.

3.4.1 Synthetic datasets

Random RBF Generator is a synthetic dataset that uses random centroids and weights to create new instances [7]. The version with concept drifts is called Random RBF Generator Drift, and we set the drifts to occur in the minority classes only. A change speed of 0.89 was chosen for the drift in the data. SEA is an artificial dataset introduced by [58]. It possesses two attributes relevant to generating samples. Let $att0$ and

---

Algorithm 5 1-NN semi-supervised learning

1: **for** i, i= 1,2, ..., n **do**
2:     labelled_samples = get_labelled(window[i])
3:     unlabelled_samples = get_unlabelled(window[i])
4:     labelled_window.append(labelled_sample)
5:     unlabelled_window.append(unlabelled_samples)
6:     **if** len(unlabelled_window) > window_size and len(labelled_window) > window_size **then**
7:         X_labelled,y_labelled = Get_labels(unlabelled_window,labelled_window)
8:         X.append(X_labelled)
9:         y.append(y_labelled)
10:         unlabelled_window = []
11:         labelled_window = []
12:     **end if**
13: **end for**
14: **function** GET_LABELS(unlabelled_window, labelled_window)
15:     **for** i, in len(unlabelled_window) **do**
16:         nearest_neighbor,distance = Get_NN(unlabelled_window[i],labelled_window)
17:         **if** distance < ϵ **then**
18:             X_labelled.append(unlabelled_window[i])
19:             Y_labelled.append(nearest_neighbor.Y)
20:         **end if**
21:     **end for**
        return X_labelled, y_labelled
22: **end function**

$att1$ be two random numbers between 0 and 10. If $att0 + att1 < 8$, then the label is 0; otherwise, the label is 1. In order to create the version with drifts, we use $att0 + att1 < 7$ for the first half of the data and $att0 + att1 < 14$ for the rest. Waveform is another synthetic dataset that uses the random differentiation of waveforms to create new instances [7].

3.4.2 Real datasets

Forest Cover originates from the UCI repository and contains cartographic attributes for predicting forest cover type, while KDDCup99 is a classical network intrusion dataset used for detecting normal connections or intrusion attacks [15]. Here, we selected ten classes with the highest numbers of instances and shuffled the data. Finally, the Gas Sensors dataset relates to six (6) gases kept at different pressures and is susceptible to concept drift [66].

Table 3.1: Number of instances, classes and percentages of instances in the classes for each dataset.

Dataset	Number of instances	classes	% of classes
Forest Cover	581011	7	48:36:6:3:2:1:0.4
Random RBF Generator	50000	5	53:19:18:7:1
Waveform	15000	3	75:15:9
SEA	30747	2	73:26
KDDCup99	100000	10	56:20:19:2:0.7:0.5:0.2:0.2:0.04
Gas Sensor	13616	6	21:21:18:13:13:11

3.4.3 Experimental results

In this section, we detail our experimental results. All experiments were done in Python while employing Scikit-multiflow [44]. The source-code and implementations for the experiments are available at GitHub[1]. All the parameters chosen for MOOB, MUOB and SCUT-DS were selected based on the recommendations of the original papers. The forgetting factors and thresholds for both IOE and ISOE were selected to be 0.9 and 0.05, respectively. Hoeffding trees [33] was chosen as the base classifier for all the models. Furthermore, the window size for ISOE was set to 500. The first 1000 instances in all the datasets were chosen as the warm-up period for all the models. These values were set by inspection.

3.4.4 Multi-class imbalanced learning

In this section, we compare our algorithms (ISOE and IOE) with SCUT-DS, MUOB and MOOB. For the comparison, as noted in chapter 2,

---

[1]https://github.com/pvafaie/IOE

the G-means metric was used, as it is a standard metric for imbalanced settings. Note that we followed the prequential, or test-then-train, learning paradigm [6]. Table 3.2 demonstrates the results of the comparisons. These results show that IOE gives the highest G-means value for all the datasets except SEA, where SCUT-DS provides the highest G-means value, and Random RBF Generator, where it comes in a close second to ISOE. These results indicate the limited usefulness of SMOTE in over-sampling minority classes. MUOB performs poorly consistently, which suggests that the amount of under-sampled data is excessive. In the next section, we will discuss the results for drifting and semi-supervised environments.

Table 3.2: G-means of algorithms for the datasets described in Section V. G-means of zero indicate that the recall for at least one class is zero.

Dataset	G-means				
	ISOE	SCUT-DS	MUOB	MOOB	IOE
Forest Cover	0.798	0.697	0.285	0.781	**0.829**
Random RBF Generator	**0.850**	0.809	0.741	0.833	**0.847**
Waveform	0.804	**0.820**	0.793	0.813	**0.820**
SEA	0.672	**0.681**	0.668	0.673	0.652
KDDCup99	0.892	0.883	0.000	0.889	**0.921**
Gas Sensor	0.604	0.495	0.214	0.580	**0.837**
AVG rank	2.33	3.08	4.83	2.83	1.91

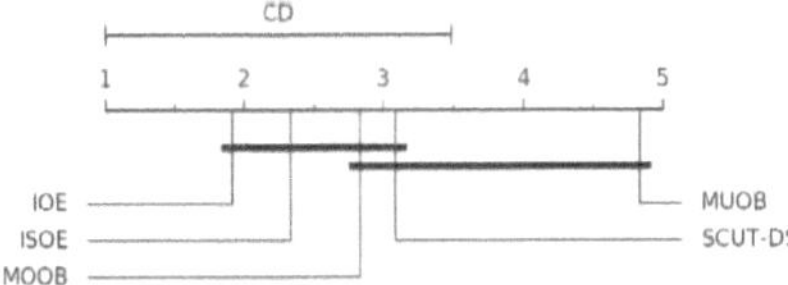

Figure 3.1: The Nemenyi test results with α set to 0.05. It can be seen that there is a statistical significance between our two algorithms with MUOB.

Table 3.3: G-means of the algorithms in the presence of concept drifts.

Dataset	G-means						
	FHDDM-confidence	DDM-OCI	DDM-minority	OzaBag-ADWIN	OzaBag	MOOB	IOE
Random RBF Generator Drift	**0.582**	0.417	0.534	0.129	0.224	0.4141	0.565
SEA Drift	0.605	0.605	**0.609**	0.152	0.131	0.577	0.605
Gas Sensor	0.771	**0.837**	0.803	0.729	0.582	0.580	**0.837**

3.4.5 Concept drift

This section compares the performance of our methodology (IOE) with those of various other methodologies when employing the concept drift algorithms described in section 3.3.2. Note that Online Bagging and Online Bagging with ADWIN are used as baselines. We chose IOE over ISOE as the model for all concept drift detection due to the higher G-means values reported for IOE in Table 3.2. Table 3.3 compares the G-means of the concept detectors for the three drifting datasets. The results imply that using concept drift detectors does not have a major effect on IOE's performance. One reason for this finding could be that IOE balances the classes' performances and thus deals with drifts on its own. As shown in [70], OOB aims to improve prediction in all the classes; by doing so, it reduces the negative effects of concept drifts. Another reason for this finding could be that by changing the performances of the classes, false drift could be triggered, resulting in too many resets of the model.

3.4.6 Online imbalanced semi-supervised learning

Finally, we compare different approaches for dealing with semi-supervised learning environments, as discussed in Section 3.3.3. The threshold for the confidence scores in self-training is set to 0.91. For 1-NN, the 0.25 quantile is chosen as the threshold for ϵ. All parameters were set by inspection. The label missing rates used in this experimental evaluation are 40%, 70% and 90%. We use IOE without any SSL as a baseline.

Table 3.4 compares the G-means values for the three methods described previously. As expected, as the percentage of unlabelled data increases, the performance of the classifier and the G-means values decrease. The G-means values are mostly higher when the 1-NN technique is used and compare well to the values found for the supervised learning setting. Notably, with 40% of the labels missing, some of the results are similar to, or even higher, than the results achieved at baseline, which could imply that the 1-NN algorithm can safely add more samples to the training set. When 90% of the labels are missing, the performances of the various approaches decrease significantly. In cases where the data contains drifts, models need more instances in order to adjust to the changing environment. Using older data or using the model trained on the instances before the drift could enforce false behavior. This enforcement could explain the significant drop in the G-means values for both the Random RBF Generator Drift and Gas Sensor datasets. However, note that, in some cases, the G-means values are higher when we do not use any pseudo-labelling, which implies that, in this scenario, we are incorrectly adding instances to the training set formed via 1-NN and confidence scores. Figure 3.2 and Figure 3.3 illustrate how the G-means values change for the Gas Sensor and Random RBF Generator Drift datasets, respectively. In Figure 3.2, note that after instance 8000, the G-means values in the self-training method decrease, which implies that false behaviors are being enforced. On the other hand, the G-means values for the 1-NN are the most stable in this particular case. In Figure 3.3, the G-means values for 1-NN are higher throughout the dataset, and the model converges faster than self-training, suggesting that 1-NN is better at adding the correct instances to the training set.

Table 3.4: G-means of the IOE model when there are missing labels. The missing rates are the percentages of instances without labels. ST stands for self-training.

Dataset	Missing rates									
	0%	40%			70%			90%		
		ST	1-NN	None	ST	1-NN	None	ST	1-NN	None
Forest Cover	0.829	0.794	**0.819**	0.780	0.731	**0.788**	0.738	0.683	**0.703**	0.685
Random RBF Generator	0.847	0.827	**0.837**	0.821	0.797	0.803	**0.813**	0.755	0.745	**0.779**
Random RBF Generator Drift	0.565	0.542	**0.607**	0.535	0.454	**0.551**	0.442	0.311	**0.435**	0.422
Waveform	0.820	0.808	**0.813**	0.809	**0.803**	0.793	0.795	0.764	0.745	**0.815**
SEA	0.652	0.641	**0.644**	0.641	**0.649**	0.635	0.643	**0.626**	0.604	0.596
KDDCup99	0.921	0.890	0.894	**0.906**	0.881	0.842	**0.898**	0.833	**0.853**	0.828
Gas Sensor	0.837	0.761	**0.839**	0.739	0.682	**0.763**	0.600	0.513	**0.692**	0.598

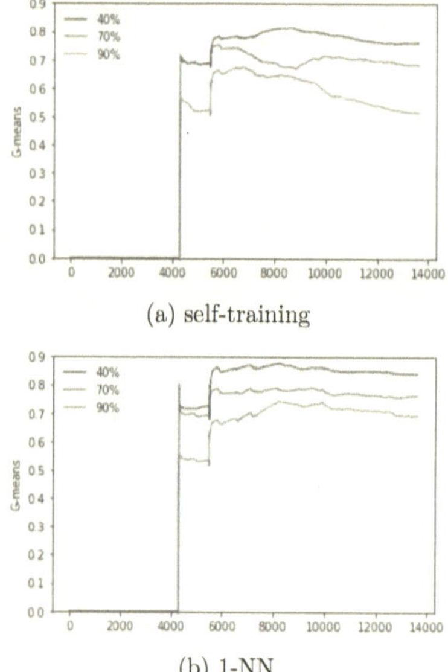

(a) self-training

(b) 1-NN

Figure 3.2: The two figures show the G-means when self-training (a) and 1-NN (b) are used in the Gas Sensor dataset with different missing rates. In (a), the confidence threshold is 0.91, whereas in (b), the threshold is the 0.25 quantile of the distances measured during the warm up period.

3.4.7 Discussion

In summary, our results suggest that IOE is able to best balance all the classes in the multi-class scenario, as was shown by its higher achieve-

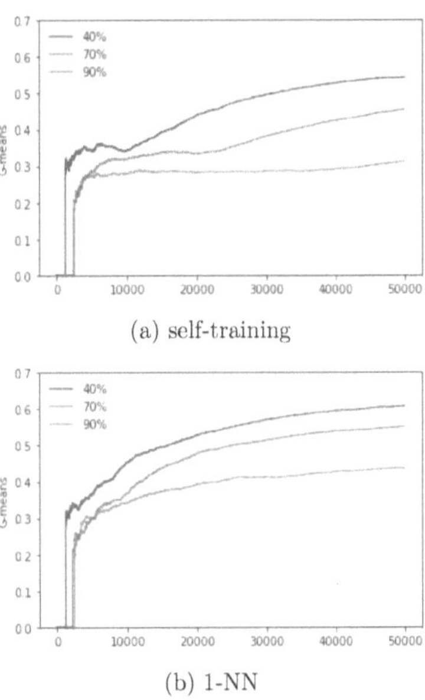

(a) self-training

(b) 1-NN

Figure 3.3: The two figures show the G-means when self-training (a) and 1-NN (b) are used in the Random RBF Generator Drift dataset with different missing rates. In (a), the confidence threshold is 0.91, and in (b), the threshold is the 0.25 quantile of the distances measured during the warm up period.

ment in terms of overall G-means values. That is, by putting greater emphasis on classes with poorer performances, IOE is able to deal with drifts in the data without relying on concept drift detectors and model resetting. ISOE and SCUT-DS, on the other hand, require more computational power and memory usage due to the overheads associated with SMOTE. Moreover, based on [17],in data streams, SMOTE-based methods create synthetic instances in an unreliable manner, which may result in creating erroneous artificial data. That is, instances in a minority class might be from multiple sub-concepts, leading to having disjuncts with few instances also defined as small disjuncts [75]. When there are insufficient instances in minority classes, the nearest neighbours of the minority instances might be from multiple small disjuncts, resulting in creating synthetic instances which could overlap other class boundaries (synthetic instances created in decision boundary of other classes). For instance, in figure 3.4, by using SMOTE, we might create instances that are between the small disjuncts, causing the synthetic instances to overlap other classes. In these methods, setting the window size to lower values might increase the chances of creating erroneous data in the minority classes, while larger window sizes might increase the time complexity and chances of mixing old and new concepts [17]. Furthermore, based on [76], setting the value for K in the K-NN method can have a major impact on the results of SMOTE-based methods in the presence of small disjuncts. Further, the results suggest that over-sampling may introduce a bias towards the minority classes, which may not be acceptable in a scenario in which all the classes are equally relevant [17]. Notably, MUOB seems to sacrifice the performances of the majority classes to improve the performances of the minority classes.

Our initial results also show that IOE potentially perform well in

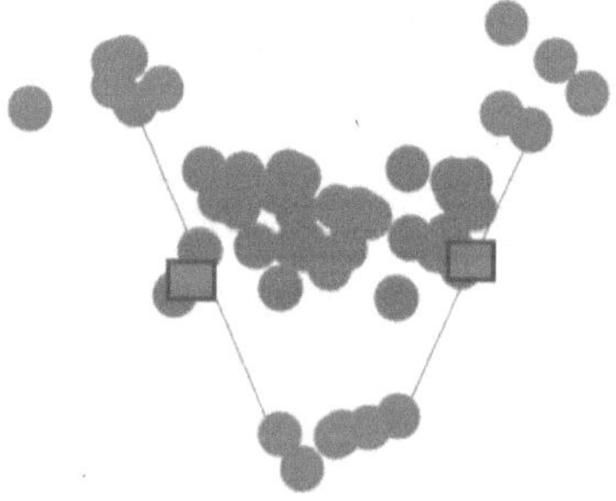

Figure 3.4: Figure demonstrating the problem of creating synthetic instances in the presence of small disjuncts [76]. In each window, having insufficient instances in the small disjuncts might result in erroneous synthetic instances in the decision boundary of other classes.

situations involving drift, which can be advantageous when dealing with real-world data with heterogeneous drifts. The concept drift detection algorithms have no clear winner, while techniques such as FHDDM, DDM-OCI and DDM all yield high results. Promisingly, IOE, without employing any explicit drift detection, also produced comparably high G-means values, an avenue we will explore in the future.

We compared two algorithms for handling missing labels in online learning. Although the 1-NN algorithm produces a better performance than the self-training with confidence scores, we acknowledge that it suffers from some drawbacks. We noticed that the performance of 1-NN depends strongly on the choice of ϵ and finding the best ϵ for each dataset is not a trivial task. The optimal value for this parameter is highly dependent on the target data. Having higher values for ϵ might result in adding incorrect pseudo-labels to the data due to the higher distance threshold, while having lower values for this parameter might result in limited pseudo-labelled data. Thus, for best results, the optimal value for the ϵ hyper-parameter should be selected based on careful consideration and experiments. In the next chapter, we introduce another method based on meta-reinforcement learning that deals with this drawback. Furthermore, the experiments on the 1-NN approach are continued in chapter 4, where this algorithm is compared with online SSL algorithms in benchmark datasets.

3.5 Summary

In this chapter, we introduced online ensembles for learning from multi-class imbalanced data and extended this work to the semi-supervised learning setting. We showed that the IOE approach produced accurate results against both static and evolving datasets. Notably, our IOE method was able to produce models with high G-means values against all classes, even in the presence of concept drift. A strength of our IOE algorithm is that it does not make any prior assumptions about imbalance rates and is thus suitable for use in cases where the rates of class instances may change, e.g., when a majority class becoming a minority class, and vice versa.

We further introduced an approach for dealing with missing labels in data-streams using one nearest neighbours. We showed that the one nearest neighbour classifier performs well when comparing against the self-training wrapper technique. An advantage of our method is that it is straightforward and fast. However, a drawback of this technique is its sensitivity to the value of ϵ and the high dependence on the correctness of the nearest neighbor's label. In the next chapter, we continue the study on online semi-supervised learning by introducing a novel approach based on meta-reinforcement learning and K-NN classifiers.

Chapter 4

Online semi-supervised learning using Deep Reinforcement Learning

In the previous chapter, we introduced the improved online ensemble approach for dealing with imbalanced data streams, that incorporated the 1-NN technique for handling missing labels. In this chapter, we continue our study by introducing the Online Reinforce SSL algorithm that utilizes meta-features to train a meta-reinforcement learning agent. The meta-features are extracted from multiple-source datasets via the predictions of various K-NN classifiers. That is, our approach uses extracted meta-features to train a meta-reinforcement (m-RL) agent to select the most appropriate predictions from the K-NN classifiers. We demonstrate that this algorithm accurately learns to distinguish between correct and incorrect predictions and show that our results outperform the current state-of-the-art.

This chapter is organised as follows. Section 4.1 introduces related work, while Section 4.2 details our Online Reinforce algorithm.Experimental evaluations follow in Section 4.3 and 4.4.

4.1 Background and related work

4.1.1 Meta-learning

Recall that meta-learning, or *learning how to learn*, is defined as training a model on source tasks to achieve generalization for new tasks. In other words, meta-learning focuses on improving the performance of a model on a new task by training the model on previous tasks. In meta-learning, it is assumed that the source and target tasks come from similar distributions of tasks $p(\tau)$ [31]. More formally, given meta-training set $\mathcal{D}_{meta-training} = \{\mathcal{D}_1, ..., \mathcal{D}_n\}$, where $\mathcal{D}_i$ is defined as the training data for task the τ_i, meta-learning leverages the $\mathcal{D}_{meta-training}$ for learning parameters θ: $P(\theta|\mathcal{D})$ that can be generalized to new tasks [18].

Meta-learning has many applications and has been successfully used in numerous domains. For instance, Fin et al. introduced a method for meta-learning called model agnostic meta-learning (MAML) [18], in which the model parameters are directly trained by gradient optimizations and adapted to new tasks via optimizations or high-tuning based on the gradient of the target task. Meta-learning has also been employed in reinforcement learning (RL) [43, 45, 52]. Applications of Meta-reinforcement learning include visual navigation [13] and learning to adapt to unexpected occurrences [45]. For instance, the authors in [13] evaluate their Meta-RL model by training it on small mazes and evaluating it on previously-unseen, larger mazes. The authors in [77] introduced an algorithm called Meta-AAD for dealing with anomaly detection using a meta-deep RL model for detecting anomalies in data streams. Their approach incorporates active learning in the labeling process [56]. Through the extraction of meta-features from data, the trained model can be transferred and applied to new datasets. Meta-RL selects possible anomalies, then the selected instances are sent to an oracle, whereas Meta-AAD outperforms state-of-the-art methods in terms of dealing with anomaly detection while reducing the false positives rates.

4.1.2 Online semi-supervised learning

Recall from chapter 2 and 3 that a number of SSL approaches are based on the so-called wrapper-based methods, such as self-training, an approach that selects the most confident predictions of a base classifier to predict labels [2, 19]. However, a major limitation of this approach is that it could emphasize false behaviour [65, 79]. Next, we briefly review the state-of-the-art in terms of online SSL.

Temporal label propagation (TLP) is an online graph-based SSL algorithm introduced in [67]. In TLP, τ unlabelled instances are propagated in a graph H by computing the harmonic solution. Although the TLP algorithm achieves good performances with a minimal number of labelled instances, traversing the graph may be prohibitive in a streaming environment.

Semi-supervised pool and accuracy-based stream classification (SPASC) uses an ensemble of classifiers introduced in [32] for dealing with online SSL. The base classifiers in SPASC are cluster-based and updated with each labelled and unlabelled batch of data. Each classifier is used to describe a single concept. When a new batch arrives, a new classifier is added to the pool if the batch contains a new concept. Otherwise, a pre-existing classifier related to the concept represented by the new batch will be updated based on this batch. There are many hyperparameters involved in SPASC, namely the batch-size, number of clusters, and method for detecting the similarity between a concept and cluster. A limitation of this approach is that clusters with similar characteristics are not merged to create larger clusters. Thus, clusters may arise that cannot perfectly distinguish between classes.

Reliable SSL (ReSSL) [57] is another cluster-based algorithm. In this method, micro-clusters are generated from labelled and unlabelled data. However, in order to deal with changes in data streams, as each instance arrives, the weights of the older micro-clusters are reduced. Online Re SSL (OReSSL) [63] extends ReSSL in that each micro-cluster's importance is based on its reliability in predicting instances. For classification, an ensemble of K-NN classifiers is used to classify each incoming instance. SPASC and OReSSL both employ unsupervised learning during the labeling process, which may result in reduced performances for some datasets, as shown in our experimental section 4.3. Next, we introduce our Online Reinforce SSL algorithm.

4.2 Online Reinforce Algorithm

Our Online Reinforce framework takes advantage of both meta-learning and reinforcement learning, as follows. Given a labelled data stream from a source domain, transferable meta-features are learned by multiple K-NN classifiers, with k ranging from 1 to K. Thereafter, meta-reinforcement learning (m-RL) is employed in order to predict the labels of unlabelled data streams pertaining to different target domains. The newly labelled instances are buffered in a sliding window of size w, allowing a base classifier to be trained incrementally. The m-RL agent may be assimilated with an active-learning oracle that can attribute labels to unlabelled instances. Our meta-features are described in the next section.

4.2.1 Meta-features

In order to be transferable, meta-features should share a common feature space and be, as much as possible, domain-independent. The meta-features employed in this work are based on the (i) Euclidean distance in the feature space between unlabelled instances and their nearest labelled neighbors, (ii) confidence scores of the K-NN classifiers, and (iii) level of agreement among classifiers.

1 – Meta-distance

Given the feature vector of an unlabelled instance and its K nearest labelled neighbors, the meta-distance is defined as

$$\chi_1\left(\mathbf{x}_u\right) = \left\{\left\|\mathbf{x}_u - k\text{-}NN\left(\mathbf{x}_u\right)\right\|_2\right\}_{k=1}^K \tag{4.1}$$

Therefore, the K nearest labelled neighbors are inferred for each unla-

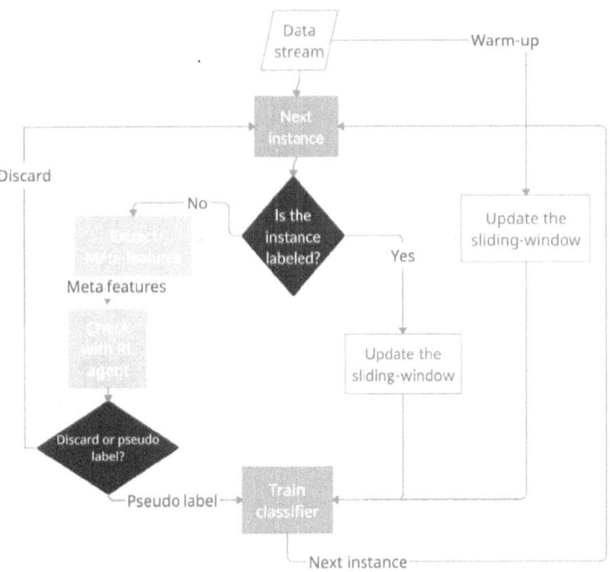

Figure 4.1: The workflow of our Online Reinforce SSL algorithm.

belled instance. Next, the Euclidean distances in between these neighbors and each unlabelled instance are evaluated. Note that these distances are not necessarily transferable from one domain to another, as the distance ranges may vary considerably. Therefore, the meta-distance defined in Eq. 4.1 is standardized by applying a z-score:

$$\chi_1 \leftarrow \left\{ \frac{\chi_{1,i} - \mu}{\sigma} \right\}_{i=1}^{|\chi_1|}, \tag{4.2}$$

where μ and σ are the mean and the standard deviation of the meta-distance features during the warm-up period. Standardization ensures that feature vectors can be transferred between domains.

2 – Confidence score

The next meta-feature consists of all the confidence scores (probabilities) attributed to the unlabelled data by the K classifiers:

$$\chi_2\left(\mathbf{x}_u\right) = \left\{ \mathrm{Pr}_{k\text{-}NN}\left(\mathbf{x}_u\right) \right\}_{k=1}^{K} \tag{4.3}$$

3 – Pairwise agreements between $k\text{-}NN$ classifiers

The various classifiers do not necessarily attribute the same label to an unlabelled instance (disagreement among classifiers). Therefore, a third meta-feature is introduced in order to consider pairwise agreements between classifiers. This feature is defined as:

$$\chi_3 = \left\{ \chi_{3,i} \right\}_{i=1}^{\binom{k}{2}},$$

$$\begin{matrix} k_1 \in [1, K-1] \\ k_2 \in [k_1+1, K] \end{matrix} : \left\{ i = 1, 2, \ldots, \binom{k}{2} \right\} : \begin{matrix} k_1\text{-}NN = k_2\text{-}NN \Rightarrow \chi_{3,i} = 1 \\ k_1\text{-}NN \neq k_2\text{-}NN \Rightarrow \chi_{3,i} = 0 \end{matrix} \tag{4.4}$$

It follows that the resulting meta-feature is obtained by concatenating the features above, that is:

$$\chi = \left\{ \chi_1 \,\|\, \chi_2 \,\|\, \chi_3 \right\} \tag{4.5}$$

4.2.2 Pseudo-labelling with meta-reinforcement learning

Meta-reinforcement learning is employed for pseudo-labelling. Initially, a sliding window of size w is filled with the first w labelled instances in the source data stream. Once the sliding window is initialized, the data stream is processed instance by instance. If a new instance is labelled, then it is added to the sliding window, and the oldest instance is discarded. Otherwise, if the instance is unlabelled, the K-NN classifiers predict its first K nearest labelled neighbors via the current sliding window. These nearest neighbors are employed to calculate the meta-features defined in Section 4.2.1. According to the meta-features, the m-RL selects the best predictions from the K-NN classifiers and assigns a label to the unlabelled instance. Subsequently, the base classifier is trained with the newly- labelled instance. If the prediction confidence level is too low, then the unlabelled instance is discarded. This approach is outlined in Fig. 4.1.

4.2.3 Training of the meta-reinforcement learning model

The training of the m-RL model is performed with data streams from multiple-source domains. Once trained, the m-RL model can be employed for pseudo-labelling in various target domains. In order to improve its robustness and generalization capability, the m-RL model is trained against several data streams in a sequential manner. Initially, meta-feature vectors are extracted from the source data streams, as described in Section 4.2.1. These data streams contain both labelled and unlabelled instances. If an instance is unlabelled, a label is assigned by the K-NN classifier following the procedure described in Section 4.2.2. The m-RL model is used to determine which classifiers are accurate when predicting labels. As there are many classifiers, the model must

---

Algorithm 6 Online Reinforce SSL Framework

```
1:  Initialize sliding-window
2:  Initialize base-classifier
3:  for (x,y) in warm-up do
4:      base-classifier.fit(x,y)
5:      sliding-window.append(x,y)
6:  end for
7:  for (x_i, y_i) in all_instances do
8:      if y_i is not null then
9:          base-classifier.fit(x_i, y_i)
10:         sliding-window.add(x_i, y_i)
11:     else
12:         all-KNNs.fit(sliding-window)                    ▷ Train all K-NN classifiers
13:         Meta-features = Obtain-Meta-features(x_i, sliding-window)
14:         action = m-RL(Meta-features)
15:         if action == discard-instance then
16:             Continue
17:         else
18:             ŷ = get-K-NN-prediction(action)            ▷ Prediction of the KNN_action
19:             base-classifier.fit(x_i, ŷ)
20:         end if
21:     end if
22: end for
```

---

be able to determine which subsets of classifiers (many classifier may converge to the same prediction) correctly predict the labels and which do not. In order to train the m-RL model, a training data stream is created. To avoid any bias toward a particular source data stream, an equal number of instances are randomly sampled from each data stream. The feature space for the training set consists of the meta-feature vectors associated with these instances. The corresponding training label space consists of binary vectors indicating which subsets of classifiers accurately predict a label: for each classifier, a value of one indicates a good prediction, while a value of zero indicates an erroneous one:

$$\psi = \{\psi_k\}_{k=1}^{K}, \quad \begin{cases} \psi_k = 1 \Rightarrow \hat{y}_{i,k} = y_i \\ \psi_k = 0 \Rightarrow \hat{y}_{i,k} \neq y_i, \end{cases} \tag{4.6}$$

where y_i is the real label associated with instance i, $\hat{y}_{i,k}$ is the label predicted by the K-NN classifier, and ψ is the so-called m-RL label; that is, the label employed to train the m-RL model. These m-RL labels should be distinguished from the original source labels. Indeed, their role is to indicate which K-NN classifiers correctly label the instances, while the original labels refer to the classes associated with the meta-feature vectors.

Recall that reinforcement learning involves four essential elements: the state S_t, the policy π_θ, the action A_t, and the reward R_t. The state consists of all extracted meta-features (Section 4.2.1). The policy, which is a learnable neural network, determines which action the agent should take to increase the expected reward. Given an unlabelled instance, the agent selects a classifier or a subset of classifiers for label prediction (recall that the m-RL label ψ allows a subset of classifiers to agree over the same label). Alternatively, it may discard an unlabelled instance if the probability associated with the action is too small. The reward is equal to one if the selected classifiers properly predict the label (positive reward), zero if the instance is discarded (neutral reward), and $-\rho$ when the prediction is incorrect (negative reward); the lower the value of $-\rho$, the greater the number of instances discarded.

Recall from chapter 2 that this problem may be formulated in terms of a Markov decision process (MDP). This process aims to maximize the expected cumulative reward given either the current state (value function) or the current state and action (value-action function):

$$V_\theta\left(s_t\right) = \mathbb{E}_t\left[\sum_{k=0}^{\infty}\gamma^k R_{t+k+1}\,|\,s_t\right] \tag{4.7}$$

$$Q_\theta\left(s_t, a_t\right) = \mathbb{E}_t\left[\sum_{k=0}^{\infty}\gamma^k R_{t+k+1}\,|\,s_t, a_t\right], \tag{4.8}$$

where θ represents the parameters of the neural network associated with the policy, $\gamma \in [0, 1]$ is a discount factor (weighting between the short-term and long-term rewards), $V_\theta(S)$ is the value function, $Q_\theta(S, A)$ is the value-action function, and $\mathbb{E}_t$ is the mathematical expectation. Reinforcement learning solves the MDP optimization problem by learning a value or a value-action function approximating the expected cumulative reward. In the present work, proximal policy optimization (PPO) is employed [55]. This policy is an actor-critic model, in which the critic estimates the value function, while the policy is inferred by the actor. The parameters are learned by minimizing a loss function consisting of three components: the actor loss function, the critic loss function, and an entropy term fostering exploration. The loss function associated with the critic is given by:

$$\mathcal{L}_t^C = \mathbb{E}_t \left[\left(V_\theta(s_t) - \hat{V}_\tau \right)^2 \right], \tag{4.9}$$

where $\hat{V}_\tau$ is an estimate of the value function based on the data. The loss function associated with the actor is the clipped surrogate objective:

$$\mathcal{L}_t^A = \mathbb{E}_t \left[\min \left(r_t(\theta) \hat{A}_t, \ \Xi \left(r_t(\theta) ; 1 - \varepsilon, 1 + \varepsilon \right) \hat{A}_t \right) \right], \tag{4.10}$$

where

$$r_t(\theta) \overset{\wedge}{=} \frac{\pi_\theta(a_t \,|\, s_t)}{\pi_{\theta^-}(a_t \,|\, s_t)}, \tag{4.11}$$

in which π_{θ^-} is the policy prior to the update, $\Xi \left(r_t(\theta) ; 1 - \varepsilon, 1 + \varepsilon \right)$ is a function that clips $r_t(\theta)$ in the interval $[1 - \varepsilon, 1 + \varepsilon]$, ε is the clipping hyperparameter, and $\hat{A}_t$ is the generalized advantage estimator [54], which is defined as:

$$\hat{A}_t \overset{\wedge}{=} \delta_t + \sum_{t'}^{T} (\gamma \lambda)^{t'} \delta_{t+t'}, \tag{4.12}$$

where $\delta_t = r_t + \gamma V_\theta(s_{t+1}) - V_\theta(s_t)$ and λ is a hyperparameter. The advantage estimator determines the efficacy of the various actions while the Ξ function ensure that the policy remains stable by impeaching large updates [55, 77]. The total loss function is presented as follows:

$$\mathcal{L}_t = \mathbb{E}_t \left[\mathcal{L}_t^A (\theta) + \mu_1 \mathcal{L}_t^C (\theta) + \mu_2 S \left(\pi_\theta \left(\cdot \, | s_t \right) \right) \right], \qquad (4.13)$$

where S is the entropy, while μ_1 and μ_2 are weighting hyperparameters. The mathematical expectation is approximated via data sampling [77]. Once the training is completed, the PPO model can be employed for pseudo-labelling in a target data stream. Algorithm 6 outlines the generation of the pseudo-labels with the trained m-RL model in a streaming environment. Our experimental results are presented in the next section.

4.3 Experimental evaluation

In this section, we describe our experimental setup. We will first detail the datasets used for the evaluation. Consequently, we will describe the state-of-the-art algorithms and the hyperparameters used for comparing the methods.

4.3.1 Datasets

Table 4.1 summarizes the data streams used in our evaluation. We employed the following synthetic datasets:

Recall that **Random radial basis function (RBF) generator** is a synthetic dataset employing random centroids for generating new instances: 50,000 instances partitioned into 50 clusters were created [7]. As noted in chapter 3, **Random RBF generator drift** is a variation of RBF featuring concept drifts. In this variation, we can choose any number of centroids to contain drifts with a change speed [7]. As in RBF, we created 50,000 instances by setting the number of centroids to 50 and setting the number of drifting centroids to 25. Furthermore, the changing speed for the drifting centroids was set to 0.1 [7].

Recall that **Waveform** is a synthetic dataset that uses waveform formulas for creating synthetic instances [7]. In our experiments, we set the number of instances to 30,000.

In addition, our evaluation also included the following real datasets:

Recall that **Gas sensor array drift (GSD)** is a multi-class dataset used to characterize the behavior of six gases at various pressures [66].

Electrical is a binary dataset that relates to whether the prices of electricity will go up or down [7].

Shuttle is an imbalanced NASA dataset containing space shuttle re-entry parameters: 80% of the instances belong to the rad flow class, while the remaining instances pertain to the remaining five classes [15].

Weather is a binary dataset containing 18,159 instances predicting whether it will rain or not.

Room occupancy aims predicting whether an office is occupied or not based on lighting, temperature, humidity, and carbon dioxide level [15].

PAMAP tracks six subjects performing 18 different activities [53].

Nursery concerns the ranking of applications for access to nurseries. It has 12,960 instances, eight features, and five classes [15].

4.3.2 SSL algorithms

Online Reinforce: For our method, we used our IOE algorithm (presented in the previous chapter) with Hoeffding trees (HTs) as base learners [7]. For the implementation of PPO, we used the stable baseline's [51] implementation with the recommended hyperparameters. Two fully-connected neural networks, each consisting of two hidden

Table 4.1: Characteristics of the data streams.

Data stream	Number of Features	Number of Instances	Number of Classes
GSD	130	13616	6
Electrical	9	45311	2
RBF	11	50000	5
RBF drift	11	50000	5
Waveform	22	30000	3
Shuttle	10	58000	7
Weather	9	18159	2
PAMAP	54	59425	6
Room occupancy	6	20560	2
Nursery	9	12959	5

layers of 64 neurons with tangent hyperbolic (*tan-h*) activation functions, were used as the network architecture in both the actor and critic models. A linear activation function was used for the output layer of the critic model, while a *softmax* activation function was used for the output layer of the actor model. The learning rate for training the neural networks was set to 0.0003, while the sliding window size w was set to 1000. Further, the value for ρ was set to 15. For each dataset, we train ORSSL based on the other datasets and set the episode length to 50000. The K-NN classifiers used were 1NN, 3NN, 5NN, and 7NN. All of the above-mentioned values were set by inspection.

OReSSL [63], introduced earlier, is a state-of-the-art method for dealing with SSL in data streams. hyperparameters were selected based on the recommended values in the OReSSL paper.

SPASC [32] is another online ensemble algorithm using cluster-based algorithms as base estimators. The batch size and the number of clusters are tuned for each individual dataset based on the values suggested in the original paper. SPASC has two modes, namely Heuristic and Bayesian. In the results section, we show the results for the mode with the highest accuracy.

1-NN is the online SSL method we introduced in the previous chapter.

Recall that this approach looks at the closest neighbour with distance closer than threshold ϵ. We set the sliding window size to 300, and set the ϵ to be the one quartile of the nearest neighbours distances in the warm-up period.

Recall that **Self-training** is a wrapper that utilizes the most confident predictions as pseudo-labels for unlabelled instances. Similar to the previous chapter, we use this method as a baseline. In our experiments, we paired self-training with IOE, HTs and Naïve Bayes algorithms and set the confidence threshold to 91%.

4.3.3 Experimental results

This section compares the results of our algorithm with those of the algorithms described in Section 4.3.2. For each dataset, we use four different unlabelled rates, namely 30%, 10%, 3%, and 1%. For all the evaluations, we used prequential test-than-train [7] to obtain the accuracy of the classifiers. Table 4.2 demonstrates the accuracies of the SSL algorithms on all the datasets.

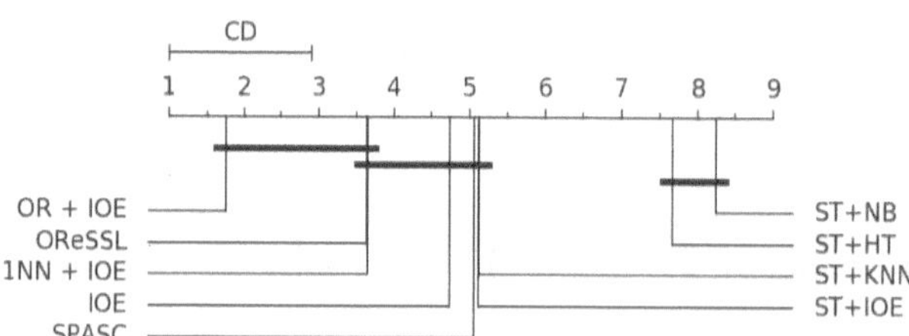

Figure 4.2: The Nemenyi test results with α set to 0.05.

Based on the obtained results, we conclude that our Online Reinforce SSL algorithm often outperforms the state-of-the-art in terms of model accuracy, with OReSSL coming in second. This is the case for all levels of unlabelled data across the target datasets. Our results also

Table 4.2: Accuracies of SSL algorithms for different label percentages. OR is shorthand for Online Reinforce, while ST stands for self-training.

Dataset	Label%	Acc								
		OR + IOE	OReSSL	SPASC	1-NN + IOE	ST+NB	ST+HT	ST + 5NN	ST + IOE	IOE
GSD	1%	57.90	**67.17**	51.20	55.65	48.99	45.63	18.59	53.41	55.65
	3%	67.01	**81.77**	63.74	57.11	49.06	50.45	36.72	56.00	55.34
	10%	77.03	**91.19**	79.10	72.94	43.31	43.31	74.29	61.40	58.99
	30%	82.98	**96.12**	87.90	80.03	53.05	53.05	89.41	76.42	70.31
Electrical	1%	72.50	66.02	67.73	72.41	45.41	65.46	61.89	64.62	**73.24**
	3%	**75.06**	69.97	69.18	75.36	47.07	70.76	64.86	72.78	74.96
	10%	**79.83**	74.32	72.63	78.62	45.58	74.56	70.94	77.40	79.32
	30%	**83.28**	80.71	78.51	82.66	55.83	74.58	78.40	82.46	82.25
RBF	1%	86.43	**91.49**	63.71	60.33	46.68	40.49	84.81	50.91	55.67
	3%	85.60	**91.48**	66.12	71.86	46.33	46.79	85.18	51.37	61.12
	10%	87.03	**91.71**	69.77	78.16	46.78	52.93	87.04	69.06	76.77
	30%	86.65	**91.86**	71.39	84.11	56.05	57.99	90.55	82.26	81.63
RBF drift	1%	**56.83**	52.42	44.88	46.65	40.73	40.73	55.35	35.53	37.84
	3%	**58.62**	56.18	47.44	53.81	41.17	41.17	56.54	47.44	40.59
	10%	**61.06**	59.10	50.05	57.48	43.80	43.80	58.85	50.32	49.88
	30%	59.65	**60.74**	53.7	57.59	47.71	47.71	61.34	56.91	54.85
Waveform	1%	**84.40**	80.12	78.46	81.58	77.20	63.49	63.56	80.92	83.45
	3%	**83.53**	83.05	80.56	81.12	77.33	67.07	68.86	79.82	82.00
	10%	**83.02**	82.47	79.82	80.65	77.71	63.76	75.76	80.56	82.37
	30%	83.08	**83.47**	78.46	82.74	78.37	74.65	81.60	82.45	81.58
Shuttle	1%	**99.19**	98.00	96.88	91.43	95.82	87.68	97.69	96.07	94.07
	3%	**99.12**	98.18	96.20	97.77	85.21	89.92	97.73	94.70	94.76
	10%	**99.18**	98.87	96.65	98.20	89.14	90.69	97.92	97.38	97.91
	30%	**99.53**	99.20	97.42	99.37	80.80	95.56	98.52	99.40	99.20
Weather	1%	**73.85**	67.35	71.80	67.53	60.26	68.51	70.03	67.49	67.53
	3%	**72.63**	66.75	70.54	68.88	60.16	68.51	70.07	57.97	67.24
	10%	71.47	**72.71**	70.58	69.71	60.17	62.95	71.84	67.65	68.66
	30%	71.21	**76.42**	71.78	72.77	60.68	68.58	74.99	70.14	70.41
PAMAP	1%	**76.76**	56.86	42.27	73.70	39.29	37.26	38.60	64.29	42.83
	3%	**83.77**	61.26	43.30	82.18	39.78	44.26	43.34	75.79	60.08
	10%	**93.94**	66.39	46.58	89.04	41.69	42.76	50.87	83.59	91.77
	30%	**97.10**	66.66	49.30	96.34	43.96	45.36	63.96	94.97	96.58
Room occupancy	1%	**98.89**	97.39	98.05	98.76	93.96	96.76	98.46	98.67	98.73
	3%	**98.90**	98.36	98.06	98.82	94.08	97.45	98.46	98.65	98.39
	10%	**98.87**	98.52	97.84	98.88	94.68	96.76	98.61	98.82	98.83
	30%	**98.89**	98.68	98.42	98.84	95.47	96.90	98.65	98.87	98.84
Nursery	1%	73.78	60.80	**81.71**	70.36	61.17	58.84	35.37	71.50	70.36
	3%	80.51	67.59	**84.59**	77.57	61.35	65.50	35.85	75.74	78.49
	10%	83.33	73.77	**86.30**	81.79	38.45	66.58	59.95	79.85	81.38
	30%	87.35	78.28	**87.65**	86.07	71.08	71.55	76.07	84.84	86.71
AVG rank		**1.75**	3.6375	5.0625	3.65	8.25	7.675	5.125	5.1125	4.7375

confirm that combining the IOE algorithm with Online Reinforce SSL benefits learning. For instance, in the PAMAP dataset with 1% labelled data, using our algorithm with IOE resulted in 76% accuracy, while the standalone IOE had a 42.84% accuracy; that is 34% improvement by incorporating IOE into Online Reinforce.

4.3.4 Discussion

Our Online Reinforce SSL algorithm produces the highest accuracy values against most datasets, which had varying percentages of labelled instances. However, OReSSL yielded the highest values for the RBF and Gas (GSD) streams, and SPASC produced slightly higher values than Online Reinforce SSL for the Nursery stream, implying that, for these datasets, clustering benefits learning. The lower accuracies obtained when employing self-training indicates that pseudo-labelling adds too many incorrect labels, which leads to a reduction in the performance of the IOE algorithm [65].

Next, we present the results of the Nemenyi posthoc test shown in Figure 4.2. This test was used to highlight the contrasts in the algorithms against all the datasets. The figure shows that there is nearly a critical difference between our Online Reinforce SSL algorithm and OReSSL with α set to 0.05. This difference can also be seen in the average ranks, which were 1.75 for Online Reinforce SSL, 3.63 for OReSSL, 3.65 for 1-NN, and 5.06 for SPASC.

Recall that the Online Reinforce SSL algorithm is a wrapper method that is meant to be paired with numerous base classifiers. When compared to other wrapper methods, such as self-training, our algorithm performs significantly better, indicating that the use of meta-features increases the percentage of correct instances added to the training set.

For instance, figures 4.3, 4.4, 4.5 depict the number of Online Reinforce SSL and self-training with 5NN labels against the PAMAP, Waveform and RBF datasets, each with 1% labelled data. The results indicate that the Online Reinforce model is clearly able to distinguish between data that can and cannot be labelled, thus leading to a reduction in the number of false positives. That is, in Online Reinforce figures, the red section is insignificant compared to the green and blue

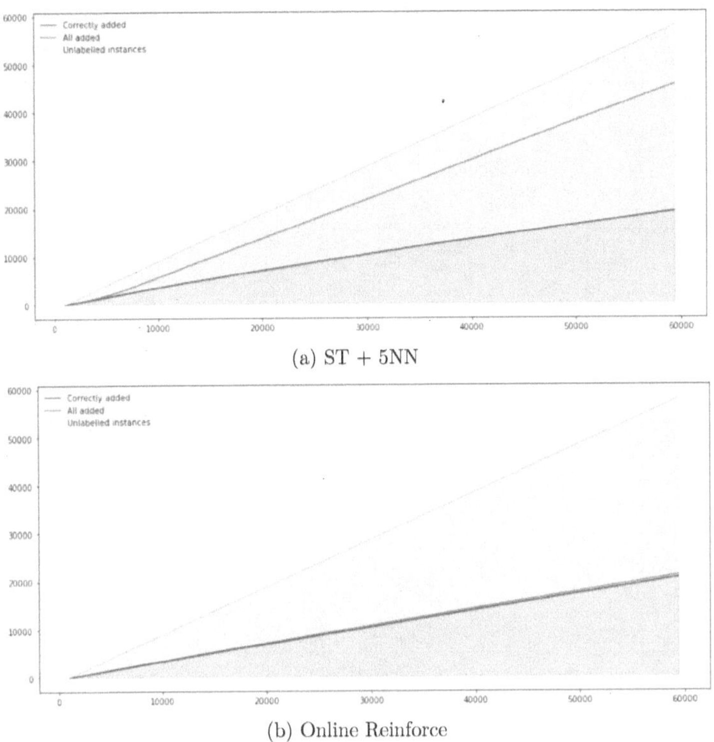

(a) ST + 5NN

(b) Online Reinforce

Figure 4.3: Number of unlabelled instances correctly labelled by the Online Reinforce SSL algorithm. compared to self-traning with 5NN in the PAMAP dataset with 1% labelled data. Green show all unlabelled instances, blue depicts correctly labelled instances, while red corresponds to instances labelled incorrectly.

sections, which confirms the value of our meta-reinforcement learning approach.

Figure 4.6 illustrates the percentage of each action selected by the Online Reinforce SSL algorithm for the PAMAP and RBF datasets with 30% unlabelled data. Note that for the PAMAP dataset, the agent mostly chose 1-NN, while for RBF, the most chosen action was 3NN. Interestingly, the percentages for the actions are different for each

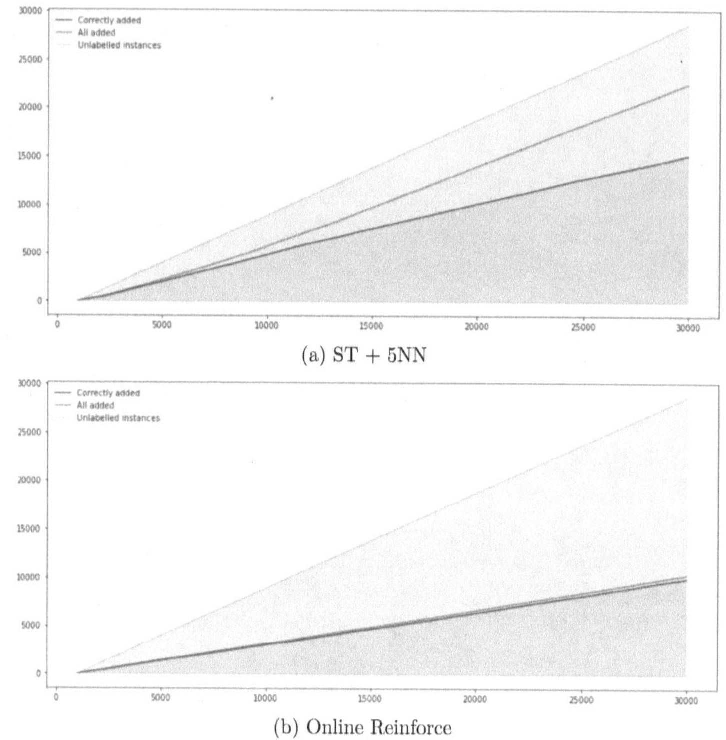

(a) ST + 5NN

(b) Online Reinforce

Figure 4.4: Number of unlabelled instances correctly labelled by the Online Reinforce SSL algorithm, compared to self-traning with 5NN in the Waveform dataset with 1% labelled data. Green show all unlabelled instances, blue depicts correctly labelled instances, while red corresponds to instances labelled incorrectly.

dataset, meaning - as may be expected - that selecting actions is dependent on the characteristics of the data.

4.4 Concept drift experiments

Recall that in many real-world situations, the distribution of data might change over time, resulting in so-called evolving or non-stationary streams. This section further continues our experiments by comparing

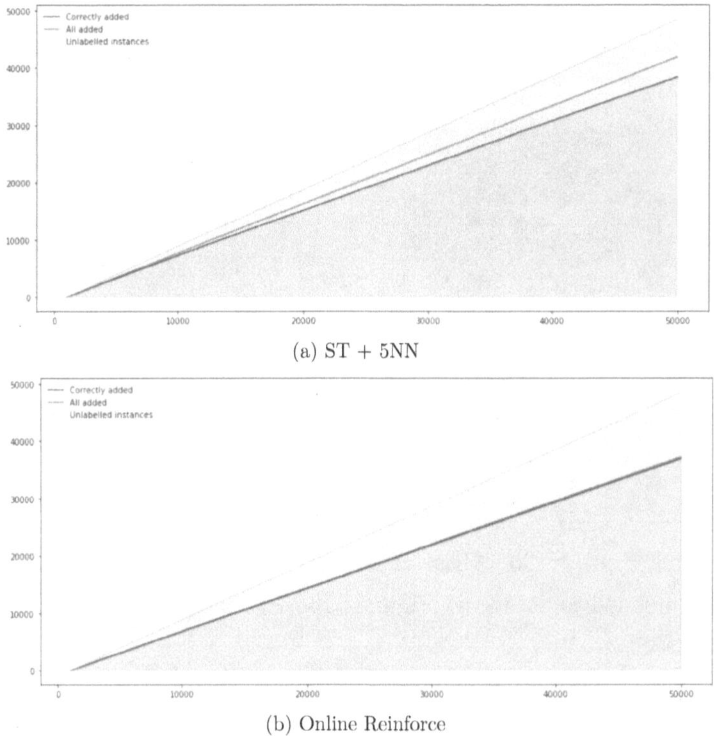

(a) ST + 5NN

(b) Online Reinforce

Figure 4.5: Number of unlabelled instances correctly labelled by the Online Reinforce SSL algorithm, compared to self-traning with 5NN in the RBF dataset with 1% labelled data. Green show all unlabelled instances, blue depicts correctly labelled instances, while red corresponds to instances labelled incorrectly.

the methods in datasets containing abrupt, re-occurring and incremental drifts. OReSSL addresses concept drift by removing older clusters and does not need to be paired with concept drift detection. Similarly, SPASC handles drifts by creating a new cluster based on new concepts. On the other hand, Online Reinforce and 1-NN do not deal with drifts and need to be paired with concept drift detectors for dealing with changes in the data. We set the batch size in SPASC to 1000 and set

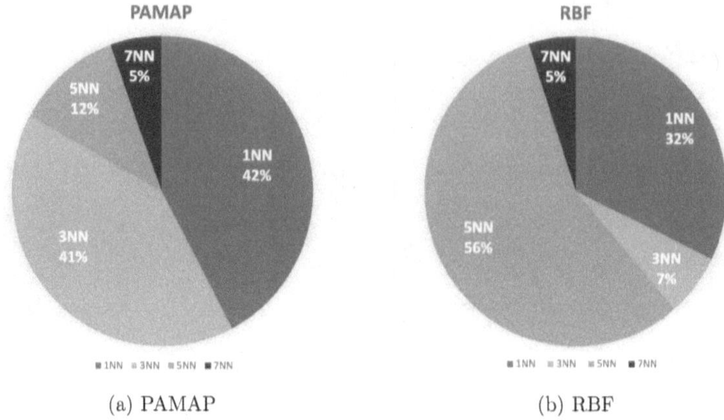

(a) PAMAP   (b) RBF

Figure 4.6: Percentages of the actions (K-NN learners) chosen by Online Reinforce SSL for the PAMAP and RBF datasets with 30% labelled data.

the cluster size to 30. These values were set by inspection. Similar to recommended values in the original paper, we set the number of clusters in OReSSL to 50.

4.4.1 Datasets

Table 4.3 summarizes the datasets used for this experiment. The following synthetic datasets with artificial drifts are used for evaluating methods in non-stationary environments:

Table 4.3: Characteristics of the synthetic data streams with artificial drifts. Re stands for re-occurring, while ab stands for abrupt drifts.

Data stream	Number of Features	Drift location	Number of Instances	Number of Classes
SEA re	3	every 15000	105000	2
SINE re	4	every 15000	105000	2
MIXED re	4	every 15000	105000	2
SEA ab	3	15000	30000	2
SINE ab	4	15000	30000	2
MIXED ab	4	15000	30000	2
Hyperplane	4	incremental	30000	2
RBF drift	10	incremental	30000	3

Recall that the **SEA** dataset is an artificial dataset that contains three attributes, two of them being relevant to the label [58]. The label for each instance is determined based on a classification function. That is, if the sum of two relevant attributes is higher than a threshold, the label is 1; otherwise, the label is 0 [11]. For the re-occurring experiment, we switch the threshold from 7.5 to 9 every 15000 instances. For the abrupt experiment, we change the threshold from 7.5 to 9 at the instance 15000.

SINE is another synthetic dataset with four attributes, of which only two are relevant [25]. The label for each instance is determined based on $y = sin(x)$. That is, if the points are below $y = sin(x)$, the label is 1, and 0 if opposite [11]. For the re-occurring experiment, we reverse the classification function every 15000 instances, and for the abrupt experiment, we reverse the classification function only once at instance 15000.

MIXED is another synthetic dataset used in our experiments. There are four relevant attributes that are associated with the label, which two of them are binary, and the other two are numeric between [0,1]. There are three conditions associated with the classification function. For each instance, if two of the conditions are true, then the label is 1; otherwise, the label is 0. The conditions are as follow: 1- first binary attribute is true, 2- second binary attribute is true, 3- $y < 0.5 + 0.3sin(3\pi x)$. For the re-occurring experiment, we reverse the conditions every 15000 instances, and for the abrupt experiment, we reverse the conditions at the instance 15000.

Hyperplane is a binary d dimensional synthetic dataset with artificial incremental drifts introduced in [34]. In this dataset, for each instance, if the $\sum_{i=0}^{i=d} w_i x_i >= w_0$, then the label is positive, and if the $\sum_{i=0}^{i=d} w_i x_i < w_0$, then label is negative. Drifts are added to the dataset by adding $d\tau$ to

w_i, where d is the change applied to the weights, and τ is the probability of changing the direction of the change [44]. In our experiments, we create 30,000 instances by setting d to 0.3 and τ to 0.5

Recall that **RBF drift** is a variation of RBF featuring incremental drifts in the data. We created 30,000 instances by setting the number of centroids to 50 and setting the number of drifting centroids to 35. We set the number of classes to three (3) and set the changing speed to 0.89 [7].

4.4.2 SSL algorithm with drift detection

Online Reinforce + DDM/EDDM

For Online Reinforce, each time DDM/EDDM signals warning in the data, we create a new sliding window and start training a new base-learner based on the incoming data. When drift is detected by the DDM/EDDM, the sliding window and the base-learner are changed to the newer versions.

1-NN + DDM/EDDM

Similarly, for the 1-NN method, when DDM/EDDM signals for warning, a new labelled sliding window and a new base-learner are created. After drift is detected, the base-learner and the labelled sliding window are updated to the newer versions.

Online Reinforce + FHDDM

We use an unsupervised approach for detecting concepts based on FHDDM [19] and confidence probabilities, which was introduced by [20]. In this approach, the confidence probabilities for each instance are estimated. When the change in the confidence scores is greater than Hoeffding bound, drift is detected, and the sliding window and the classifier are reset.

1-NN + FHDDM

Similarly, we use the same unsupervised drift detection method with the 1-NN algorithm. That is, when the distribution of confidence estimates is changed, drift is detected, and the sliding window and the base-learner are reset.

Blind Adaptation

For this method, we assume that there are drifts in the data, and blindly reset the sliding window and the base classifier every M instances. For the experiments, we set the M to 5000 for each dataset. This value was set by inspection.

4.4.3 Experimental result

This section compares the results of the online SSL algorithms paired with the concept drift detectors mentioned previously. Similar to section 4.3.3, the labelled rates are set to 30%, 10%, 3% and 1%. We also compared the results of drift detection methods in cases of 100% labelled data, i.e. for fully labelled datasets. Table 4.4 depicts the accuracies of the results.

OReSSL performs well when there are abrupt drifts in the data. However, in cases of re-occurring drifts, the results for OReSSL are behind other methods. This can be seen in MIXED, SINE and SEA with 1% labelled data and re-occurring drifts, where the results of OReSSL is nearly 10% lower than the other methods. SPASC performs well in the datasets with re-occurring concepts, such as SINE, being second after the Online Reinforce with blind adaptation.

The best results from Online Reinforce were obtained from pairing with the blind adaptation, which may be noticed in the SINE and MIXED dataset results with re-occurring drifts. Specifically, Online Reinforce with blind adaptation performed better than other drift detectors in cases of only 1% labelled data. This is evident in the Hyper dataset with 1% labelled data, where the results of Online Reinforce with blind adaptation outperforms the results of Online Reinforce with other drift detectors. Online Reinforce with FHDDM performed best in cases with a higher percentage of labelled data but performed poorly when labelled data were scarce, notably for SINE, and MIXED with 1% labelled data with abrupt drifts, where Online Reinforce with FHDDM performed worse than the other methods. 1-NN had the best performance when it was paired with the FHDDM drift detection method in almost all datasets. Both Online Reinforce and 1-NN performed worse when they were paired with the EDDM method in re-occurring datasets. For instance, the reader will notice that the results of Online Reinforce paired with EDDM is nearly 10% lower than Online Reinforce paired with DDM in the SEA dataset with re-occurring drifts.

Furthermore, we observed that the results of Online Reinforce improved significantly in almost all datasets when paired with drift detection methods, compared to Online Reinforce as a standalone. However, this difference is less noticeable in cases of 100% labelled data.

We further expanded the experiments by combining drift detectors with blind adaptation. That is, for each drift detection method, we also blindly reset the sliding window every 5000 instances. Table 4.5 demonstrates the results of the drift detection methods paired with the blind adaptation. From these results, it can be noticed that the results of Online Reinforce paired with drift detection methods have increased significantly. For instance, the results for Online Reinforce paired with DDM have improved drastically in the SINE and SEA datasets with abrupt drifts.

Moreover, we compared the results of the Online Reinforce and Online Reinforce with DDM and blind adaptation in the benchmark datasets from table 4.1, shown in Table 4.6. From these results, it can be understood that using drift detection improved the results in the Electrical and Nursery datasets, but reduced the performance on other datasets.

Table 4.4: Accuracies of SSL algorithms with DDM, EDDM and FHDDM drift detector for different label percentages. OR is shorthand for Online Reinforce, while BA is shorthand for Blind Adaptation. In cases of 100% labelled data, there is no pseudo-labelling performed by Online Reinforce and 1-NN algorithms.

Dataset	Label%	Acc									
		OR+IOE+DDM	OReSSL	SPASC	1-NN+IOE+DDM	OR+IOE+EDDM	1-NN+IOE+EDDM	OR+IOE+FHDDM	1-NN+IOE+FHDDM	OR+IOE+BA	OR+IOE
SINE re	1%	68.36	56.00	72.40	57.49	74.92	66.36	64.00	64.00	**78.29**	56.13
	3%	51.82	77.71	85.99	70.63	47.23	67.61	75.25	69.05	**86.28**	55.36
	10%	75.55	80.47	89.45	73.81	69.59	71.34	85.49	84.82	**91.38**	49.33
	30%	86.78	83.82	94.21	86.81	75.72	72.75	93.29	93.35	**94.48**	71.99
	100%	85.78	90.16	**96.95**	85.78	74.74	74.74	96.42	96.42	96.67	83.40
SEA re	1%	82.70	75.27	69.61	72.69	73.23	69.89	**82.86**	72.53	72.18	82.80
	3%	**82.84**	77.36	76.15	79.03	72.29	68.53	**82.86**	78.04	79.84	82.69
	10%	82.72	**85.01**	78.97	82.12	70.75	67.23	82.65	82.21	83.84	82.79
	30%	83.67	**87.19**	81.68	82.91	71.84	66.28	83.72	83.34	86.01	83.80
	100%	83.96	**87.53**	85.62	83.96	70.67	70.67	84.08	84.08	85.08	84.08
MIXED re	1%	69.72	56.66	52.09	57.99	47.68	63.92	54.44	66.27	**78.26**	55.43
	3%	54.80	67.48	77.24	65.72	77.57	73.09	71.22	69.61	**85.78**	54.18
	10%	67.02	80.62	80.44	71.60	76.78	72.09	79.97	81.55	**89.87**	48.13
	30%	80.03	88.00	86.09	81.52	77.67	73.40	87.64	89.49	**91.92**	72.82
	100%	86.24	**93.52**	91.19	86.24	75.87	75.87	89.29	89.29	92.95	82.62
SINE ab	1%	47.75	71.11	74.13	57.49	74.25	50.24	47.69	68.00	**81.65**	47.66
	3%	48.02	74.64	83.44	70.63	76.25	77.50	48.00	70.38	**88.31**	47.67
	10%	72.06	83.25	89.10	73.81	75.68	83.30	78.26	81.70	**92.15**	67.24
	30%	89.21	90.46	91.82	86.81	77.16	73.21	92.92	**95.78**	94.76	84.04
	100%	95.43	86.45	95.11	95.43	75.55	75.55	96.70	96.70	**96.83**	92.37
SEA ab	1%	81.03	64.14	72.75	79.62	78.32	70.25	81.36	**84.14**	75.04	81.04
	3%	81.84	79.61	78.50	79.03	74.75	70.37	81.39	**83.51**	80.09	81.46
	10%	85.90	**87.13**	81.31	82.12	71.18	69.27	84.95	83.91	84.05	85.14
	30%	87.760	**91.78**	81.49	82.91	70.56	66.74	87.38	85.53	86.19	87.67
	100%	87.64	**87.68**	85.25	87.64	72.69	72.69	87.00	87.00	85.66	87.00
MIXED ab	1%	47.67	68.72	**80.75**	57.99	47.78	57.74	56.43	60.58	78.84	47.47
	3%	48.26	**86.84**	81.83	65.72	80.08	60.00	62.27	58.63	85.83	48.40
	10%	69.88	88.53	81.82	77.60	85.33	73.91	84.34	87.81	**89.98**	68.13
	30%	86.48	92.04	80.21	81.52	77.06	77.74	**92.60**	90.82	91.99	83.47
	100%	93.13	**95.57**	88.98	93.13	75.67	75.67	88.34	88.34	92.88	88.11
Hyper	1%	29.38	75.09	**77.58**	41.17	29.46	44.77	29.23	61.03	78.39	28.85
	3%	75.99	76.21	**84.82**	66.21	75.03	74.88	49.34	74.87	82.61	37.92
	10%	78.13	84.83	85.03	79.59	76.37	75.33	77.42	81.32	**86.15**	66.42
	30%	87.07	86.53	86.60	**89.34**	79.37	74.45	86.39	84.49	88.66	81.47
	100%	90.49	88.32	87.56	90.49	79.52	79.52	90.02	90.02	**91.60**	86.89
RBF drift	1%	33.86	**38.10**	34.48	34.03	47.78	34.34	33.47	33.93	32.81	33.98
	3%	33.37	**38.00**	35.60	34.93	34.83	33.35	34.63	35.63	34.59	34.31
	10%	36.20	**38.71**	37.48	37.28	34.14	35.05	36.02	36.37	34.34	36.75
	30%	37.62	**40.86**	37.49	39.91	35.64	35.05	36.59	36.93	35.37	40.77
	100%	36.91	**43.43**	39.25	36.91	35.86	35.86	40.11	40.11	36.73	42.69

4.4.4 Discussion

In the previous section, we demonstrated the results of SSL algorithms when there are abrupt, re-occurring and incremental drifts in the data. SPASC performed well in the re-occurring datasets, showing that SPASC can effectively create a classifier for each concept present in the data and use it in the future when the same concepts are presented again. On the other hand, OReSSL performed poorly in datasets with re-occurring drifts, which could be due to the elimination of the oldest micro-clusters. However, OReSSL performs significantly better in

Table 4.5: Accuracies of SSL algorithms with DDM, EDDM and FHDDM drift detectors, while blindly resetting the window every 5000 for different label percentages. OR is shorthand for Online Reinforce, and BA is shorthand for Blind Adaptation. In cases of 100% labelled data, there is no pseudo-labelling performed by Online Reinforce and 1-NN algorithms.

Dataset	Label%	Acc									
		OR+IOE+DDM	OReSSL	SPASC	1-NN+IOE+DDM	OR+IOE+EDDM	1-NN+IOE+EDDM	OR+IOE+FHDDM	1-NN+IOE+FHDDM	OR+IOE+BA	OR+IOE
SINE re	1%	68.36	56.00	72.40	62.66	68.77	66.36	58.78	64.00	**78.29**	56.13
	3%	75.22	77.71	85.99	71.31	75.29	67.61	79.58	75.25	**86.28**	55.36
	10%	83.79	80.47	89.45	80.67	75.90	71.34	87.40	86.32	**91.38**	49.33
	30%	85.03	83.82	94.21	89.11	75.20	72.75	92.94	93.29	**94.48**	71.99
	100%	85.78	90.16	**96.95**	85.78	74.74	74.74	96.42	96.42	96.67	83.40
SEA re	1%	**81.59**	75.27	69.61	77.97	73.07	69.89	81.17	74.52	72.18	82.80
	3%	**83.77**	77.36	76.15	82.00	76.16	68.53	80.27	81.86	79.84	82.69
	10%	**84.25**	85.01	78.97	82.40	79.95	67.23	83.46	82.26	83.84	82.79
	30%	85.23	**87.19**	81.68	84.12	72.64	66.28	83.91	83.47	86.01	83.80
	100%	83.96	**87.53**	85.62	83.96	70.67	70.67	84.08	84.08	85.08	84.08
MIXED re	1%	69.72	56.66	76.15	61.50	74.25	63.92	66.08	66.27	**78.26**	55.43
	3%	79.72	67.48	77.24	73.45	74.97	73.09	77.38	74.51	**85.78**	54.18
	10%	84.69	80.62	80.44	75.67	76.31	72.09	82.78	81.93	**89.87**	48.13
	30%	86.68	88.00	86.09	81.31	76.29	73.40	88.86	89.31	**91.92**	72.82
	100%	86.24	**93.52**	91.19	86.24	75.87	75.87	89.29	89.29	92.95	82.62
SINE ab	1%	**83.42**	71.11	74.13	57.12	75.25	50.24	48.53	68.00	81.65	47.66
	3%	85.57	74.64	83.44	76.57	78.67	77.50	77.91	81.30	**88.31**	47.67
	10%	87.29	83.25	89.10	80.49	79.20	76.88	87.96	83.16	**92.15**	67.24
	30%	89.94	90.46	91.82	88.20	75.64	73.2	94.65	**95.42**	94.76	84.04
	100%	95.43	86.45	95.11	95.43	75.55	75.55	96.70	96.70	**96.83**	92.37
SEA ab	1%	82.96	64.14	72.75	83.64	73.63	70.25	82.55	84.14	75.04	81.04
	3%	**84.10**	79.61	78.50	82.23	72.29	70.37	84.52	84.58	80.09	81.46
	10%	86.64	**87.13**	81.31	83.70	71.75	69.27	85.21	83.79	84.05	85.14
	30%	87.76	**91.78**	81.49	82.23	70.84	66.74	86.58	86.06	86.19	87.67
	100%	87.64	**87.68**	85.25	87.64	72.69	72.69	87.00	87.00	85.66	87.00
MIXED ab	1%	82.47	68.72	80.75	55.35	82.79	57.74	56.43	60.58	78.84	47.47
	3%	81.62	**86.84**	81.83	73.74	78.37	80.33	62.27	78.88	85.83	48.40
	10%	83.68	88.53	81.82	86.02	85.33	73.91	84.34	86.04	**89.98**	68.13
	30%	90.27	92.04	80.21	83.35	77.091	78.59	**92.60**	91.47	91.99	83.47
	100%	93.13	**95.57**	88.98	93.13	75.67	75.67	88.34	88.34	92.88	88.11
Hyper	1%	80.03	75.09	77.58	41.17	70.66	44.77	30.58	61.03	78.39	28.85
	3%	81.95	76.21	**84.82**	73.45	77.29	74.88	57.89	75.03	82.61	37.92
	10%	85.43	84.83	85.03	79.28	77.79	75.33	77.00	82.26	**86.15**	66.42
	30%	87.75	86.53	86.60	**88.69**	79.80	74.45	86.09	85.68	**88.66**	81.47
	100%	90.49	88.32	87.56	90.49	79.52	79.52	90.02	90.02	**91.60**	86.89
RBF drift	1%	35.38	**38.10**	34.48	34.03	34.95	34.34	33.98	33.97	32.81	33.98
	3%	35.39	**38.00**	35.80	34.97	34.02	33.35	35.54	35.13	34.59	34.31
	10%	**39.48**	38.71	37.48	37.37	34.52	34.06	35.80	33.62	34.34	36.75
	30%	40.58	**40.86**	37.49	40.14	34.45	34.43	40.16	35.11	35.37	40.77
	100%	36.91	**43.43**	39.25	36.91	35.86	35.86	40.11	40.11	36.73	42.69

datasets with abrupt and incremental drifts due to effectively removing older and least effective micro-clusters.

In terms of drift detection methods, due to too many false drift detections, EDDM performed worst comparing to other methods. This is evident from the results of Online Reinforce and 1-NN, which are the lowest when paired with EDDM. Online Reinforce obtained the best results when paired with blind adaptation, especially in cases with 1% labelled data. This could be due to late or missing drift detections for other methods. That is, in cases of 1% labelled data, drift detection algorithms did not detect drift in time for resets in the model, which resulted in adding incorrect instances by the Online Reinforce method. Another reason for this could be that these methods detect too many false drifts in certain situations, resulting in redundant model and slid-

Table 4.6: Accuracies of Online Reinforce as with and without drift detections on the benchmark dataset. The drift detection methods are blind adaptation (BA), and DDM mixed with blind adaptation.

Dataset		Acc		
	Label%	OR+IOE	OR+IOE+DDM	OR+IOE+BA
GSD	1%	**57.90**	53.34	43.93
	3%	**67.01**	61.41	59.79
	10%	77.03	**79.49**	70.70
	30%	**82.98**	76.55	74.40
Electrical	1%	72.50	**72.73**	66.71
	3%	75.06	**76.36**	72.22
	10%	79.83	**80.12**	76.65
	30%	83.28	**84.45**	82.40
RBF	1%	**86.43**	46.63	36.31
	3%	**85.60**	53.07	48.53
	10%	**87.03**	50.58	63.81
	30%	**86.65**	53.10	67.52
RBF drift	1%	**56.83**	56.75	29.85
	3%	**58.62**	57.08	37.08
	10%	**61.06**	51.11	47.65
	30%	**59.65**	44.41	48.69
Waveform	1%	**84.40**	78.86	64.30
	3%	**83.53**	79.54	73.39
	10%	**83.02**	79.64	79.15
	30%	83.08	**83.39**	81.77
Shuttle	1%	**99.19**	93.45	71.44
	3%	**99.12**	97.70	84.83
	10%	**99.18**	97.58	92.39
	30%	**99.53**	97.63	94.94
Weather	1%	**73.85**	70.85	62.60
	3%	**72.63**	70.57	63.49
	10%	**71.47**	68.11	66.11
	30%	**71.21**	70.45	66.66
PAMAP	1%	76.76	**78.81**	28.44
	3%	**83.77**	52.03	42.47
	10%	**93.94**	43.99	59.00
	30%	**97.10**	40.63	75.94
Room occupancy	1%	**98.89**	98.87	93.82
	3%	**98.90**	98.83	96.55
	10%	**98.87**	98.83	97.54
	30%	**98.89**	98.88	98.42
Nursery	1%	73.78	**75.94**	60.18
	3%	**80.51**	79.39	73.94
	10%	**83.33**	82.62	81.46
	30%	87.35	**88.46**	84.82

ing window resets.

We noticed that by combining the drift detection algorithms with blind adaptation, the results improved. That is, the results of drift detections are more stable in the 1% labelled data. FHDDM with confidence estimates and blind adaptation performed best when we had more than 10% labelled data. However, when there are 1% labelled data, the results of Online Reinforce and 1-NN paired with FHDDM are considerably lower than the other methods. This suggests that in cases of scarce labelled data, confidence estimates might not be stable, which would result in too many false drift detections. DDM with blind adaptation had the most stable results when compared to the other drift detection methods. That is, we can see that, unlike FHDDM, the results of Online Reinforce paired with DDM and blind adaptation do not change significantly as the percentage of labelled data decreases.

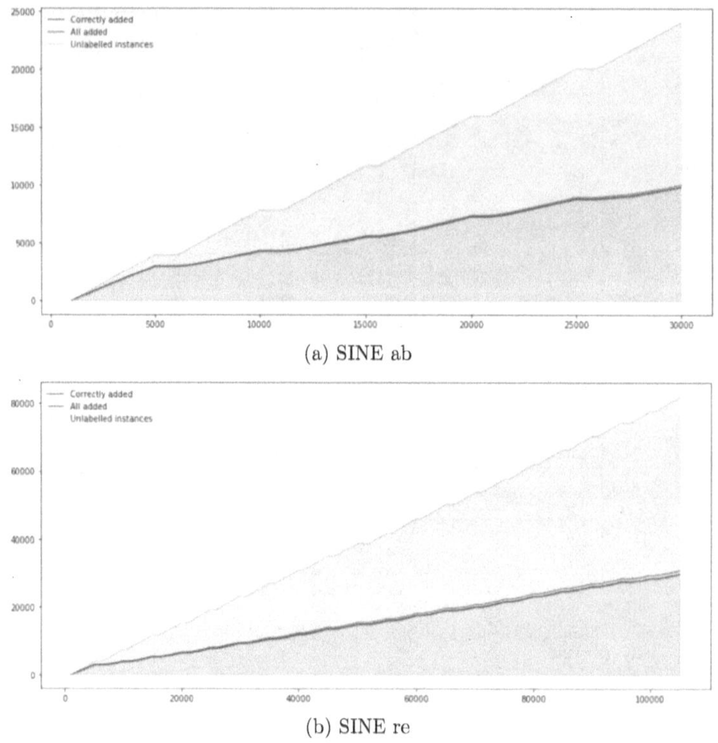

(a) SINE ab

(b) SINE re

Figure 4.7: Number of unlabelled instances correctly labelled by the Online Reinforce with DDM drift detector in (a) SINE dataset with abrupt and (b) SINE dataset with re-occurring drifts with 1% labelled data. Green show all unlabelled instances, blue depicts correctly labelled instances, while red corresponds to instances labelled incorrectly.

Furthermore, from table 4.6, the results of Online Reinforce decreased significantly when paired with drift detectors. This could be due to many false detections and resets caused by the DDM method. Using blind adaptation also reduced the results of Online Reinforce in almost all datasets. This implies that resetting the model every 5000 is redundant, as the distribution of these datasets might not change over time. However, we believe that more study is required to adapt our system in drifting scenarios without compromising performance.

Finally, figure 4.7 demonstrates the number of correct instances labelled by the Online Reinforce with DDM and blind adaptation on the SINE dataset with abrupt and re-occurring drifts with 1% labelled data. From this figure, it can be noticed that although there are multiple changes in the distribution of data, Online Reinforce can effectively add correct instances to the training while minimizing false information.

4.5 Summary

This chapter introduced the Online Reinforce methodology for dealing with missing labels in data streams. Our algorithm employs K-NN classifiers to construct meta-features that subsequently act as input to an m-RL agent, thus enabling our online learning algorithm to select the most appropriate pseudo-label for an unlabelled instance as it arrives in the stream. A crucial component of our approach is the fact that learning of the meta-RL agent is occurring across multiple domains while using transferable meta-features. We compared our Online Reinforce method with state-of-the-art Online SSL approaches and showed that our algorithm consistently yielded promising results for numerous benchmark data streams. We further continued the experiments by comparing methods in drifting environments. We demonstrated that by pairing our algorithm with drift detection methods, we achieved promising results in data streams containing abrupt, re-occurring drifts, and incremental drifts. We also showed that more research is needed for efficient drift detection in semi-supervised learning environments.

Chapter 5

Conclusion and future work

Learning from evolving data streams that are prone to skewed class distributions and lack of labels is an important emerging area of research in the online learning community. In the literature, these research questions are often handled separately, which hinders the applicability in real-world domains. In this **book**, we addressed the combined challenge when learning from imbalanced non-stationary streams where the number of labels may be scarce. Our first objective was to introduce algorithms that maintain high performance across all classes, and especially the minority classes, in a multi-class learning setting. Second, we addressed the issue of learning with missing labels, by the development of an efficient algorithm for use in domains where the number of labels may be very low (1%).

Next, we summarize the contributions of this **book**.

5.1 Contribution

5.1.1 Online imbalanced learning

We introduced the improved online ensembles algorithms for dealing with online multi-class class imbalanced. We showed that by balancing the performance over all the classes, the IOE approach produces accurate results against both static and evolving datasets. That is, even in the presence of concept drift, the IOE method was able to generate models with high G-means values across all classes.

Furthermore, our algorithm has the advantage of not requiring prior assumption about imbalance rates, making it ideal for use in cases where the rates of majority and minority classes may change. That is, by incorporating the online class recalls and class sizes, IOE maintains the rates of the classes in an online manner and adapts the sampling process accordingly.

5.1.2 Online semi-supervised learning

This **book** further introduced the Online Reinforce methodology for dealing with missing labels in data streams. Our Online Reinforce algorithm consists of a meta-reinforcement learning model that selects the best prediction from K-NN classifiers. Specifically, K-NN classifiers are used to construct meta-features that subsequently act as input to an m-RL agent, thus enabling our online learning algorithm to select the best pseudo-label for an unlabelled instance as it arrives in the stream.

To deal with the challenges of training a model in real-time, the learning of the meta-RL agent is occurring across multiple domains while using transferable meta-features. That is, the meta-reinforcement learning model is trained on multiple domains and transferred to the target domain for pseudo-labelling.

The Online Reinforce method was compared to state-of-the-art online SSL algorithms. In our experiments, we showed that Online Reinforce consistently yielded promising results for numerous benchmark data streams.

The novelty of our Online Reinforce approach is the use of a meta-RL model for selecting instances. That is, traditionally, wrapper methods (such as self-training and co-training) need a fixed confidence threshold for determining instances for pseudo-labelling, which results in possible false pseudo-labels and enforcement of erroneous behaviour [79]. However, in our methodology, instead of employing a confidence threshold, we extract meta-features and use a meta-RL model for effectively selecting instances for pseudo-labelling. The experimental evaluation and results show that the meta-RL greatly reduces the amount of possible false pseudo-labels, especially when compared to confidence thresholds used in other, older wrapper methods. On the other hand, cluster-based approaches such as OReSSL and SPASC create clusters of both labelled and unlabelled instances and cannot be paired with different algorithms, while our approach may be wrapped around numerous methods. Such an innovative and dynamic wrapper approach is highly suitable for improving the results of models in cases of scarce labelled data. Potential applications of our Online Reinforce framework may be found in numerous domains, such as network intrusions, detecting fraudulent transactions and health domains where the label for all instances might not be readily available.

We further extended our experiments to include synthetic data streams with artificial concepts and drifts. We paired our method with concept drift detectors and demonstrated its value in such environments. However, more research is needed for dealing with concept drifts, which will be described in the next section.

5.2 Future work

The limitations of our work are as follow. Although our improved online ensemble framework achieved excellent results in multi-class imbalanced data streams, there are drawbacks that need to be addressed in the future. We noticed that in data streams with a large number of classes, both IOE and ISOE may be computationally expensive. In our future work, we aim to address this issue by computing the size and recall of classes more efficiently.

We demonstrated the results of Online Reinforce SSL in numerous stationery and non-stationary data streams. In our future work, we plan to investigate the use of the Online Reinforce SSL algorithm in cases of highly imbalanced domains. We conclude that Online Reinforce might be biased towards the majority classes in such environments, which needs to be addressed in our future work.

Furthermore, Online Reinforce may also be extended to address additional challenges in data streams. The promising results of training a meta-reinforcement learning model may open a new door to solving the challenges involved in training Deep Learning and Reinforcement Learning models in data streams. We believe that the Online Reinforce framework can be extended to address other challenges in data streams that require instance selection, such as anomaly and novelty detection or concept drift detection. That is, the Online Reinforce algorithm may be extended to have a separate agent solely for detecting concept drifts. This agent can have separate meta-features, which could involve probability estimates, error estimates, as well as changes in the distribution of the data. We anticipate that by utilizing another agent for detecting concept drift, our extended framework may yield excellent results in fast-evolving streams.